To

....

From

....

Occasion

....

Date

....

Candle
BIBLE
STORIES
For
Every Day

CANDLE
BOOKS

Text copyright © 2006 Lion Hudson plc.
Illustrations copyright © Bill Noller International Publishing
This edition copyright © 2006 Lion Hudson plc / Bill Noller
International Publishing

Illustrations by Alan Parry and Fred Apps

Published in the UK in 2006 by Candle Books
(a publishing imprint of Lion Hudson plc).

Distributed by Marston Book Services Ltd,
PO Box 269, Abingdon, Oxon OX14 4YN

Worldwide co-edition organised and produced by
Lion Hudson plc, Mayfield House, 256 Banbury Road,
Oxford OX2 7DH,England.
Tel: +44 (0) 1865 302750   Fax: +44 (0) 1865 302757
Email: coed@lionhudson.com
www.lionhudson.com

Printed in Thailand

Contents

THE NEW TESTAMENT

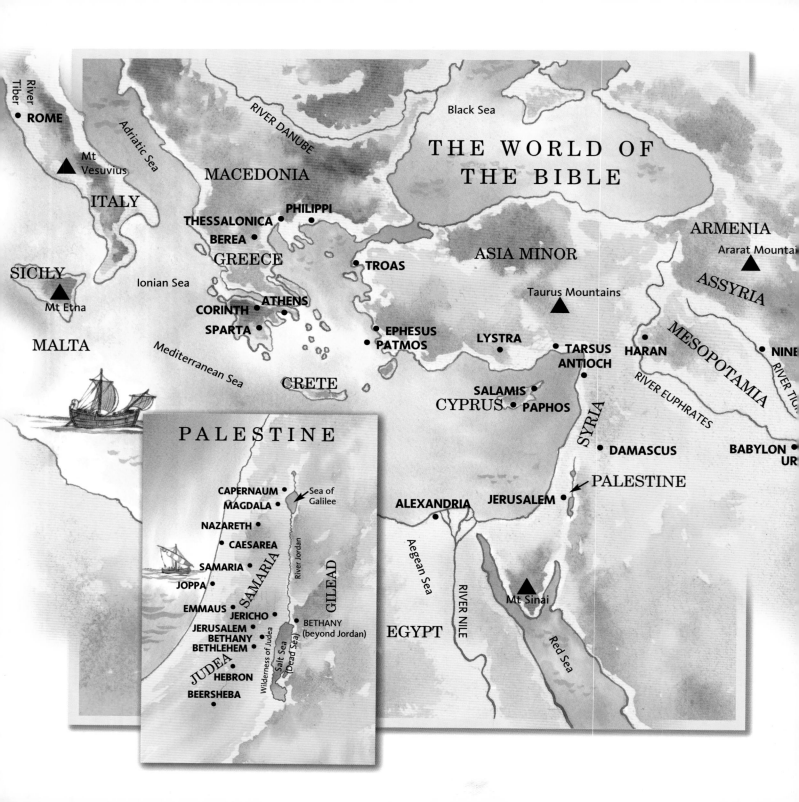

THE WORLD OF THE BIBLE

River Tiber
ROME
Mt Vesuvius
Adriatic Sea
ITALY
MACEDONIA
RIVER DANUBE
Black Sea
ARMENIA
Ararat Mountains
ASSYRIA
PHILIPPI
THESSALONICA
BEREA
GREECE
ASIA MINOR
Taurus Mountains
SICILY
Mt Etna
Ionian Sea
TROAS
MESOPOTAMIA
MALTA
Mediterranean Sea
CORINTH
ATHENS
SPARTA
EPHESUS
PATMOS
LYSTRA
TARSUS
ANTIOCH
HARAN
NINE
RIVER EUPHRATES
RIVER TIG
CRETE
SALAMIS
CYPRUS
PAPHOS
SYRIA
BABYLON
UR
DAMASCUS
PALESTINE
ALEXANDRIA
JERUSALEM
Aegean Sea
RIVER NILE
EGYPT
Mt Sinai
Red Sea

PALESTINE

CAPERNAUM
Sea of Galilee
MAGDALA
NAZARETH
CAESAREA
SAMARIA
River Jordan
SAMARIA
GILEAD
JOPPA
EMMAUS
JERICHO
JERUSALEM
BETHANY
(beyond Jordan)
BETHANY
Wilderness of Judea
BETHLEHEM
Salt Sea (Dead Sea)
JUDEA
HEBRON
BEERSHEBA

THE OLD TESTAMENT

13

DAY 1

The World is God's Creation

Genesis 1–2

A long time ago, God made the world. It was dark and empty, and nothing lived in it. Then came six days of Creation. This is what happened. On the first day God said, "Let there be light," and light came. God called the light day. At the end of the day, darkness returned, and God called it night.

On the second day God placed the sky above the earth and called it heaven.

On the third day God divided the water-covered earth into rivers, lakes, and oceans. He made dry land appear between them. Then he made plants grow on the land. On the fourth day God made the big bright sun to shine during the day. He made the moon and sparkling stars to shine at night.

On the fifth day God made fish and other sea creatures. Then he made waterbirds, like ducks and geese, and other birds, like robins and eagles, that live high in the trees. On the sixth day God made animals.

He made huge ones, like elephants, and tiny ones, like mice. Some were beautiful, like the tiger. Others were funny looking, like the anteater. Some, like the cheetah, could run fast. Others, like the turtle, walked very slowly. And God made insects – some that flew, some that crawled, and some that jumped.

A Good Man in a Sinful World

Genesis 6

As time went on, people became more and more sinful. They didn't care about pleasing God or obeying him. God kept warning them, but they didn't pay any attention. This made God very angry. He said, "I am going to destroy them by sending a great flood of water to cover the earth. Everyone will drown, all the people, animals, snakes, birds, and insects – everything."

But there was one man, Noah, who loved God and served him. God wanted to save Noah and his family from the Flood. He told Noah to build a very large boat, as high as a three-story house, with a long window reaching all around it, just under the roof.

The boat would be big enough for Noah, his wife, their three sons, Shem, Ham, and Japheth, and their wives. It would also have room for many animals – at least two of every kind, as well as birds, reptiles, and insects.

Noah Obeys Orders

Genesis 7

Noah did exactly what God told him. He built the boat, sometimes called an ark, and made it as long, as wide, and as high as God had said. It took him about a hundred years.

When the ark was finished, God told Noah to gather the animals and food for many weeks. Noah was to take a male

and a female of some kinds of animals so babies would be born. Of other kinds he was to take seven pairs – some for eating and some for sacrificing when they could leave the ark.

Noah obeyed God's instructions. He took his family and the animals into the ark. About a week later, the Flood began. Rain poured down, and the floodwaters rose up until there was enough water to make the huge ark float. Every creature left outside the ark drowned – men, women, and children, animals, birds, reptiles, and insects.

But because Noah and his family had obeyed God's warning, they were safe inside the ark, floating on top of the water.

A Long Boat Ride

Genesis 8

Rain kept falling for more than a month, but Noah and his family stayed dry inside their boat. They must have been glad that they had listened to God and obeyed him! Finally the rain stopped, and very slowly the water began to go down again. Noah and his family stayed inside the ark for 150 days. By that time the water had gone down enough for the boat to touch the ground, up in some mountains called Ararat. Still they stayed inside, waiting for God to tell them when it was safe to get out.

Noah sent a raven out of the boat. It kept flying around until the ground became dry. Then he sent out a dove. The dove came back, so Noah waited for about a week and then sent it out again. This time it returned carrying an olive leaf in its bill, showing that the water had gone down to the level of the trees. After another week he sent the dove out once more, and this time it didn't come back. In a few more weeks the ground became dry enough to walk on. Then God said, "Noah, it is time to leave the boat."

26

Dry Land at Last

Genesis 8–9

Noah let all the animals, birds, snakes, and insects out of their stalls and cages onto the dry ground. Then Noah and his family left the ark too. First of all Noah and his sons built an altar and worshipped God. They thanked him for saving them from the Flood. They sacrificed some of the extra animals they had taken onto the boat. God was happy that they wanted to worship him, and he was pleased with their sacrifice. God said to himself, "Although people will disobey me again, I will never send another flood."

God told Noah and his sons to have many children so the earth would again be full of people. He said they would be able to use animals and other creatures for food and for doing work.

Then God told Noah about his decision not to use a flood again to wipe out the people and animals on earth. He said, "When it rains, don't be afraid of another flood, but look up at the sky. There you will see a beautiful rainbow. It will remind you of my promise to you and to your children after you."

DAY 11

The Tower of Babel

Genesis 11

After the Flood ended, Noah's sons had many children and grandchildren. Sadly, they did things that displeased God just like the people who had lived before the Flood. Nowadays people speak many different languages, but in Noah's day everyone spoke the same language. They wanted to live together and decided to build a huge tower that would reach up into the sky. They said, "This tower will show how great we are. We can stay together and not get spread out across the earth."

This was against God's command to occupy the earth and take care of it. God was displeased when he saw the tower they were building. He decided to stop them by making them speak in different languages so they couldn't understand one another! This made them angry, and they gave up trying to work together, leaving the tower unfinished. The tower is called the Tower of Babel. Babel means "mixed-up" or "confused". The languages were mixed up and so were the people! Finally, small groups who could speak to each other moved away from the ones who spoke other languages, and so the people scattered to all parts of the earth.

DAY 12

Abram Believes God

Genesis 12

Long ago a man named Abram lived in a large city. Abram and his family believed in God, but their neighbours worshipped idols. One day God told Abram to leave his home and go to a special country that would belong to him and his children. That country was Canaan, and because God promised it to Abram, we call it the Promised Land. Abram believed God, so he took his wife, Sarai, and his nephew, Lot, and they started to Canaan. Abram also had many servants and animals. Having many animals was like having lots of money – so Abram was very rich.

When they got to Canaan, God said to Abram, "I'm going to give this land to you and to your children forever." Abram thanked God by building an altar and sacrificing an animal on it.

But there was a famine in Canaan. A famine is when crops don't grow because there isn't enough rain, and many people starve to death. Abram took Sarai, Lot, and his servants into Egypt, where there was enough food. When the famine was over, they returned to the Promised Land to live.

DAY 13

A Selfish Choice

Genesis 13

Abram had very large herds and flocks of cows, sheep, and goats. Lot had many animals too. They had servants who took care of their animals, but the two groups of servants quarrelled about the best fields and the best water supply for the animals.

When Abram heard this, he said to Lot, "This is a large country. I will divide the land with you. Then our shepherds won't have to fight over the pasture and the water. Lot, you may have the first choice."

Abram could have kept the best land for himself because God had given it all to him. But he was generous. His nephew, Lot, was not as kind. He chose the best part, close to the river Jordan, where the fields were well watered. But when he chose that part, he also chose to live in the wicked city of Sodom. Later on Lot's selfish choice caused much trouble.

A Wonderful Promise

Genesis 13

After Lot had moved away, God made some more wonderful promises to Abram. "Look around you. I am going to give you and your children all the land you can see. Someday even the land Lot chose will be yours too.

And I will give you many children, grandchildren, and great-grandchildren. You will have as many descendants as there are bits of dust on the earth. They will become a great nation, and I will bless them."

That promise has come true. Today we call that great group of people the Jews or Israelis, and the Promised Land, Israel.

Abram moved to Hebron and built another altar to the Lord. Each time he moved, he built a new altar so he always had a place near him where he could worship God by making sacrifices.

Lot is Captured

Genesis 14

About that time, four neighbouring kings made war against Sodom. They won and stole all the money, food, clothing, and jewellery in Sodom. They took some people to become their slaves. Lot was one of them. When Abram heard that Lot was in trouble, he gathered his servants and friends and chased after the army. They caught up with the four kings and started to fight. God let Abram win. He rescued Lot and the other captives.

As they

32

The people in Zoar weren't much better than the ones in Sodom, and Lot became afraid of them. He decided he would be safer in the mountains, so he and his daughters lived in a cave. His daughters were not good women. They became the mothers of men who started very wicked tribes that made a lot of trouble for God's people many years later.

The Son of Promise

Genesis 21

The following year Sarah had a baby boy. At last Abraham had the son who would start the great nation God had promised him. Abraham and Sarah remembered God's instructions and named the baby Isaac.

Isaac grew, and Abraham gave a party for him. Ishmael, Abraham's older son, who had been born to Hagar, the servant woman, was at the party. He teased his half brother, Isaac, and this made Sarah angry. She told Abraham he should send Hagar and Ishmael away. Even though it had been Sarah's idea that Abraham have a baby with Hagar, the servant-wife, Sarah had always been jealous of Hagar and Ishmael.

Ishmael was not the son of God's promise, but he was Abraham's little boy, and Abraham didn't like to send him away. God said to Abraham, "Let the boy and his mother go, and I will take care of them. Ishmael, too, shall become a great nation."

So Abraham gave Hagar and Ishmael food and water and sent them into the desert.

DAY 22

God Takes Care of Ishmael

Genesis 21

As Hagar and Ishmael walked through the desert, they quickly used up the water Abraham had given them. Hagar didn't know where to find any more water. She was afraid that Ishmael would die of thirst.

She found a bush. Ishmael lay down in its shade. Then Hagar walked away and sat by herself, crying. Ishmael was crying, too, because he was so thirsty. Then the Angel of the Lord said to Hagar, "God has heard your son crying. Don't be afraid. Go back and comfort him." As she was returning to Ishmael, suddenly she saw a well! She filled up the water bottle and gave Ishmael a drink. He felt better, and they were able to continue their trip.

They made their new home in Paran. Ishmael grew up and became an expert with a bow and arrow. He married a girl from Egypt, and they had many descendants who became a great nation, as God had said they would. Just as Ishmael didn't get along well with Isaac, so Ishmael's descendants, the Arabs, have never got along well with Isaac's descendants, the Jews.

DAY 23

Abraham Proves His Faith

Genesis 22

One day God told Abraham to take Isaac up to Mount Moriah and offer him as a burnt sacrifice on an altar. Although Abraham loved his son very much, he obeyed. He took Isaac and two servants and started up the mountain, carrying

40

a knife, some wood, and some fire to light the wood. When they could see the place of sacrifice ahead, Abraham left the servants, and he and Isaac went on. Isaac asked Abraham, "Father, where is the lamb we are going to offer?"

Abraham answered, "God will give us the lamb for sacrifice, my son."

When they arrived, Abraham built an altar and arranged the wood on it. Then he tied Isaac up and laid him on the wood. He raised the knife to kill Isaac, but at the last moment the Angel of the Lord said, "No! Don't hurt your son. I can see that you really do love and trust me. You were even willing to give me your precious son of promise."

Just then Abraham saw a ram caught in a bush nearby. He sacrificed the ram to God and named that place The Lord Will Provide. They returned home. Abraham had passed God's test, and Isaac was spared.

Isaac Needs a Wife

Genesis 24

Sarah died several years after Isaac was born. Abraham and Isaac missed her very much. Isaac was now a grown man and was thinking about getting married. Abraham didn't want him to marry one of the women who lived in Canaan because they didn't love and worship God. So he decided to send his oldest, most trusted servant to look for a wife for Isaac. Abraham had many relatives where he used to live, and among them would be the right wife for his son.

The servant said, "If the woman won't come here, shall I take Isaac back there to marry her?"

"No!" Abraham answered. "God told me that this is where we should live, and Isaac must stay here. If she won't come, I will forgive you for being unable to keep the oath you are making. But please try to bring back a good wife for Isaac."

The servant promised to follow Abraham's instructions. He took many fine gifts with him and set out for the place where Abraham's relatives lived.

The Right Wife for Isaac

Genesis 24

The servant arrived at Nahor's village and stopped near a well. As he watched the women come to draw up water, he asked God to help him find a good wife for Isaac. He decided on a test. He would ask one of them to give him a drink of water. If she said yes and offered to water the camels, too, she would be the right one.

A beautiful young woman came to the well and filled her water pitcher. Abraham's servant asked her, "May I please have a drink?"

"Yes, sir. And I will be glad to draw water for your camels, too." And she kept drawing up water until the camels had had enough.

She had passed his test, so the servant offered her some of the gifts he had brought and asked her who she was. Her name was Rebekah. She was the daughter of Bethuel, a son of Nahor, which meant she was Abraham's grandniece and Isaac's cousin! The servant asked if he might stay overnight at her home because he wanted to ask her family to let her marry Isaac. Then he thanked God for helping him find Rebekah.

43

God Answers a Prayer

Genesis 24

Rebekah hurried home to tell her family about the man at the well. Her brother, Laban, invited the visitor to their home, and the servant told them his story.

They listened, amazed, when he said he was their uncle Abraham's servant from Canaan. He told them he had prayed that God would lead him to the right wife for Isaac. He said he had tested Rebekah, and she was the one he was looking for.

Rebekah's father and brother said, "We can see that God brought you here. You may take Rebekah to be Isaac's wife."

The servant thanked God. Then he gave Rebekah and her family the rest of the gifts. He wanted to leave the next morning, but her mother and brother, Laban, said, "We want her to stay with us a few more days. But we'll ask her what she wants to do." Rebekah said she would go at once, so her family gave her their blessing. When they got to Canaan, the servant told Isaac the story of how he had found Rebekah. Rebekah became Isaac's bride, and he loved her very much.

Esau Throws Away Something Valuable

Genesis 25

Rebekah had twin baby boys, Esau and Jacob. Esau was the older one, so he received the birthright. That meant that when his father died, Esau would receive most of the family money and land. The younger twin, Jacob, would get only half as much.

When they grew up, Esau became a skilful hunter. He would kill wild deer for food. Isaac liked that deer meat, called venison. He especially loved Esau. Jacob was quieter and preferred to stay at home. He was Rebekah's favourite son.

One day Jacob was cooking a big pot of stew. Esau came in from hunting, tired and hungry. He said, "Let me have some of that. It smells good."

Jacob saw a chance to cheat Esau. "All right, I will if you give me your birthright."

Esau said, "The birthright won't do me much good if I starve to death! You may have it." So Esau had a good supper. He was so hungry he didn't even care that he had traded something of great value for just a bowl of stew.

DAY 28

Jacob Fools His Father

Genesis 27

Isaac was getting old, and he was almost blind. He asked Esau to go hunting and bring back a deer. "Cook the meat the way I like it, and I will ask God to bless you."

Rebekah heard Isaac say this. She wanted Jacob to

45

receive Isaac's blessing, so she thought of a way Jacob could trick Isaac. She cooked two young goats so that they tasted just like venison. When they were ready, she told Jacob to take them to his father.

"But Esau has a lot of hair on his arms and chest, and I don't. Father will know I'm not Esau."

So Rebekah tied some of the goatskin around Jacob. He took the meat to his father.

Isaac said, "Your voice sounds like Jacob's. Let me feel you to be sure you are Esau." He felt the goatskins on Jacob's arms and was satisfied. He ate the food and gave Jacob the blessing he had promised Esau.

When Esau came back and cooked the venison for his father, Isaac realized that Jacob had tricked him. It was too late. He had already given Jacob the special blessing.

DAY 29

Rebekah Helps Jacob Escape

Genesis 27

Esau saw how much he had lost through his own thoughtlessness and Jacob's trickery. He was furious with Jacob. "He got my birthright," he growled, "and now he has stolen my blessing. As soon as our father dies, I'm going to kill him."

Rebekah heard about Esau's threat. She told Jacob, "Your brother hates you. Go to Haran and stay with my brother, Laban, until Esau cools down. I will let you know when it is safe to return."

Esau was married to two Canaanite women who didn't love God, and this made his parents very unhappy. To get Isaac to let Jacob go to Haran, Rebekah said, "We don't want Jacob to marry one of the girls around here like Esau did, do we?"

Isaac agreed. He told Jacob to go to his grandfather Bethuel's home and find a good wife among Rebekah's relatives. This was just what Rebekah had wanted him to say. Isaac blessed Jacob and told him he would someday inherit the land of promise, as God had promised Abraham and Isaac before him.

Then Jacob quickly packed up and left.

A Stairway to Heaven

Genesis 28

Jacob travelled toward Haran. That night he slept on the ground with a stone for a pillow. He dreamt of a stairway reaching from earth to heaven. Angels were walking up and down it.

Then he saw the Lord, who said, "I am the God of Abraham and Isaac. You will be a part of the great nation I promised them. You will have many children, and this land will be yours forever. I will take care of you wherever you go. One day I will bring you back to this land. I'll never leave you."

Jacob woke up excited and afraid because God had come to him in a dream. He got up and worshipped God at an altar he made by setting up the stone he had used as a pillow. He poured oil over it as an offering. Jacob named that place Bethel, which means "the house of God".

Then Jacob made a very serious promise. He promised that if God took care of him and brought him back to the Promised Land, he would always love and trust God. "I will worship you and give you one-tenth of everything you give me."

Jacob Marries Leah and Rachel

Genesis 29

When Jacob got to where his mother's relatives lived, he met his cousin Rachel at the well. She was Laban's younger daughter. Jacob helped her water her sheep.

Then he told her who he was. She told her father, and Laban welcomed Jacob.

Jacob stayed with Laban's family and helped with his sheep. After about a month, Laban said, "You shouldn't work for nothing. Tell me what payment you want."

Jacob was in love with Rachel. He told Laban he would work for him free for seven years if Laban would let him marry Rachel. Laban agreed. After seven years, it was time for the wedding.

When the wedding feast was over, Laban brought Jacob's bride to his tent after dark. When he woke up in the morning, Jacob found that Laban had tricked him and given him Rachel's older sister, Leah, whom he didn't love. He was angry, so Laban said, "It was important that the older girl be married first. You may have Rachel, too, if you will work for another seven years." Jacob agreed.

50

Jacob's Secret Escape

Genesis 29–31

Leah's servant girl was called Zilpah, and Rachel's, Bilhah. Jacob married both of them, too. His four wives bore him many sons, but his favourite was Rachel's son Joseph. Jacob wanted to go back to Canaan, but Laban didn't want him to leave. Jacob said, "I'll stay if you will give me some sheep and goats so I can have flocks of my own."

Laban agreed, and soon Jacob's flocks grew very large, making him a rich man. Laban's sons became jealous of Jacob and his wealth. Jacob realized he would have to leave Haran secretly. He and his wives took all Jacob's flocks and everything they owned and left very quietly one day when Laban was out shearing his sheep.

Three days went by before Laban knew they were gone. He followed Jacob, and when he caught up with them, he said he just wanted to say goodbye to his daughters and his grandchildren. They camped together overnight, then said goodbye. On the way to Canaan, Jacob saw some angels, so he knew God was with him.

Jacob Wants Peace with Esau

Genesis 32

Jacob wondered how Esau would feel about his coming back. It had been twenty years since Jacob had tricked Isaac and stolen Esau's blessing. Was Esau still angry with him? Did he still want to kill him? Jacob decided to send messengers to Esau to tell him he was coming and that he wanted to be friends.

The messengers came back and said, "Esau is coming out to meet you, and he has four hundred men with him." That really scared Jacob! He divided his family, servants, and flocks into two groups. If Esau should attack, at least one group might be able to escape. Next, Jacob prayed that God would protect him from Esau's anger. He thanked God for all the good things that had happened to him in Haran.

Then Jacob gathered several hundred of his animals as a gift for Esau. He sent servants ahead with the animals to meet his brother. He thought it might make Esau less angry with him. Maybe they would be able to be friends after all.

DAY 34

Jacob Prepares to Meet Esau

Genesis 32

Jacob wanted to protect his wives and children in case there was fighting when he met Esau. So for safety, he sent them across the river Jordan. When he returned to his camp, a man came and started wrestling with him. They wrestled until early morning. When the man saw that he could not overcome Jacob, he put Jacob's hip out of joint.

The man said, "It is morning; let me go now."

Jacob answered, "No, not until you bless me."

"What is your name?" the man asked.

Jacob told him.

"I'm going to change your name to Israel, which means 'one who struggles and prevails with God.' You will also be strong and prevail with men."

Jacob asked the man his name. The man would not tell him, but he gave Jacob the blessing he had asked for. Jacob knew then that the man was the Lord in the form of a man. Jacob named the place where they had wrestled, Peniel, which means "the face of God". He said, "I saw God face-to-face, and yet my life was spared."

God Cares for Jacob

Genesis 33

The moment came for Jacob and Esau to meet. Jacob went on ahead of his family, and as he came close to Esau, he bowed down to show his respect. Esau ran to meet him and hugged and kissed him. They were so glad to see each other that they both cried for joy.

When Esau saw Jacob's large family, he asked, "Who are all these women and children with you?"

Jacob replied, "These are the children God has given me."

Esau asked, "And why did you send all those animals to me?"

Jacob said, "I sent them as a gift – to make you feel friendly toward me."

Esau said, "I have all the flocks and herds I need. You keep them." But Jacob insisted, and finally Esau accepted them.

Esau offered to travel with Jacob the rest of the way, but Jacob

53

was still a little afraid of him. He told Esau to go on ahead and he and his family would follow more slowly.

So God answered Jacob's prayer and reunited him with Esau, and the brothers could be friends after twenty years apart.

DAY 36

The Death of Isaac

Genesis 33–35

Jacob travelled toward Canaan. He camped at Succoth, then entered Canaan and stayed at a city called Shechem. He bought a piece of land and built an altar. He called it "God, the God of Israel."

Then God sent him to Bethel to build an altar. Jacob knew Bethel well because he had dreamed about the stairway to heaven there and God had promised to bring him back safely.

Jacob built a great altar and made sacrifices to show God how grateful he was for his blessings. God reminded him about his new name, "Israel", and about the great nation he had promised Abraham.

On the way to Bethlehem, Rachel had another baby boy, Benjamin. After the baby was born, Rachel died. Jacob was terribly sad because he had loved her so much. He went on to see his father, Isaac, who was now very, very old. When Isaac died, Jacob and Esau buried him where Abraham and Sarah were buried.

Esau took his family and moved to Edom, where his flocks would have more pasture. Jacob and his twelve sons stayed in the Promised Land.

Joseph the Dreamer

Genesis 37

Because Jacob loved Rachel best, her son Joseph was his favourite child. Jacob gave Joseph special privileges and gifts, like a beautiful colourful robe. This made the other sons angry and jealous of Joseph.

One day, when Joseph was seventeen years old, he told his brothers about a dream he had had in which their bundles of grain bowed down to his bundle of grain. It made the brothers angry. "If you think we would ever bow down to you, you can forget it!" they growled. Now they hated Joseph even more.

Later Joseph had another dream, which he described to his family. "I dreamed that the sun and the moon and eleven stars were bowing down to me," he said. Jacob scolded him. "Do you think your mother and I and your brothers will actually come and bow to you?"

Joseph's older brothers continued to be jealous and hateful toward him. Jacob thought a lot about Joseph's strange dreams and wondered why his son dreamed such things.

Joseph Visits His Brothers

Genesis 37

Jacob's sons took care of all his flocks and herds. One day they took the animals to Shechem to find good pasture. Jacob sent Joseph to find them and bring back news about them. Joseph wandered around the fields, hunting for them, but he couldn't find them.

He met a man who said, "Jacob's sons? I heard them say they were going to Dothan." So Joseph followed them to Dothan.

When his brothers saw him in the distance, they groaned. "Look who's coming. It's the dreamer! Let's get rid of him for good. We'll kill him and toss him into a well and tell father that a wild animal ate him."

The oldest brother, Reuben, didn't like the idea of killing his young brother. He said, "Let's put him into a dry well. Maybe he'll die in there without our having to hurt him ourselves." Reuben thought that later he could secretly rescue Joseph.

When Joseph arrived, his brothers grabbed his colourful coat. They threw him into an empty well – and then sat down to eat their lunch.

Joseph's Brothers Get Rid of Him

Genesis 37

While Reuben was busy elsewhere, a caravan of camels came by. Some Ishmaelites were going to Egypt. Judah had an idea. "Listen," he said, "instead of killing Joseph, let's sell him to these traders. They will pay us and take him away so he can't bother us anymore."

So they pulled Joseph out of the well and sold him to the traders for twenty pieces of silver. The traders went on toward Egypt. Soon Reuben came back to camp and looked for Joseph, but he was gone.

Reuben was terribly upset. "What are we going to tell our father? He will be brokenhearted if Joseph doesn't return with us." They decided to let Jacob think Joseph had been killed by a wild animal. They killed a goat and put a lot of its blood on Joseph's beautiful coat. They returned to Jacob and said, "We found this robe on the ground."

"It's Joseph's coat. He must have been attacked by a wild beast and torn to bits. My dear son is dead!" Day after day Jacob grieved for Joseph. He said, "I will be sad about his death all the rest of my life."

Joseph Goes to Jail

Genesis 39–40

The traders took Joseph to Egypt and sold him to Potiphar, an officer in the king's army. In Egypt the kings were called "Pharaoh". Potiphar was the captain of Pharaoh's bodyguards. Joseph worked in Potiphar's home, and he did so well that Potiphar trusted him with more and more important jobs.

But Potiphar's wife liked Joseph too much. She tried to get Joseph to make love to her. Joseph knew this was very wrong, so he refused. She was furious and told lies about Joseph to get him into trouble. Potiphar believed her lies and threw Joseph into prison.

Joseph worked so well in prison that the chief jailer put him in charge of the other prisoners.

Pharaoh's baker and butler, the man who served his wine, were in the same jail as Joseph.

One night these men had strange dreams, and Joseph was able to tell them what their dreams meant. The baker was executed, but the butler was allowed to go back to the palace, just as Joseph had said. Joseph said to the butler, "When you get out of prison, please ask the king to let me out too." Unfortunately, the man forgot all about Joseph.

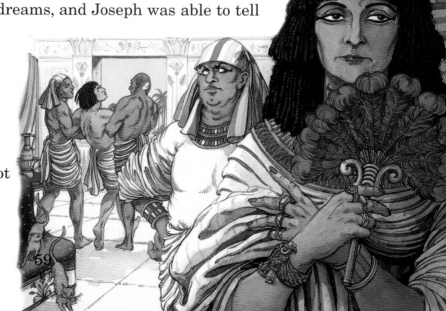

Pharaoh's Dreams

Genesis 41

Two years passed, and still Joseph was in prison. One night Pharaoh had a dream. He saw seven fat cows come out of the Nile River. Then seven thin cows came and ate up the fat ones. The king woke up, then fell asleep again and had another dream. This time he saw seven good ears of corn growing on a cornstalk. Then seven withered ears appeared and ate up the good ears. Pharaoh woke up worried.

He asked his wisest men what the dreams meant, but they didn't know. Then the butler remembered Joseph and said, "When I was in prison, I knew a man who could tell what dreams meant."

Pharaoh sent for Joseph immediately and told him his dreams. He asked Joseph what they meant. Joseph said, "I don't interpret dreams by myself; my God helps me understand them." Then Joseph said the dreams meant there would be seven good years, with plenty of food followed by seven bad years, when the crops wouldn't grow.

Joseph suggested that the king put someone in charge of storing up corn during the good years so there would be enough to eat during the bad years. The king said, "Good! You are the right person for the job!"

Jacob Moves to Egypt

Genesis 45–46

Pharaoh heard that Joseph's brothers were there. He told them to take plenty of grain back to their father and said, "Bring Jacob and your families to Egypt to live. I'll give you the best land in the whole country."

Joseph sent his brothers back with grain and many gifts for everyone. Benjamin was given more than anybody else. The brothers returned to Jacob and told him that Joseph was alive and was a great ruler in Egypt. At first Jacob couldn't believe it. But when he saw Joseph's gifts and heard about Joseph's life in Egypt, he began to realize it was true!

They packed up and set out for Egypt. Along the way God spoke to Jacob, "Don't be afraid to go to Egypt. This is part of my plan. I'll be with you, and I will bring you back home again. And when you die, Joseph will be with you."

Because Jacob's new name was Israel, the Bible calls his family and descendants "Israelites". Another name for them is "Jews". Jacob and sixty-six Israelites travelled from Canaan to Egypt. Joseph and his two sons made a total of seventy.

DAY 49

A Happy Family Reunion

Genesis 46–47

When Jacob and his family got as far as Goshen, he sent Judah on ahead to let Joseph know they were coming. Joseph hurried out to meet them. Joseph and his father hugged each other and cried for a long time. Jacob said, "Now I will be able to die happy because I have seen you again!"

Joseph introduced five of his brothers to Pharaoh. "My brothers are shepherds, and they have brought many flocks and herds from Canaan."

The brothers asked the king, "May we live in Goshen, where our flocks will have plenty to eat?" They wanted to live in Goshen because people in most parts of Egypt didn't like shepherds and wouldn't welcome them.

Pharaoh said, "Yes, if Goshen is where you want to live, you are welcome to make your home there. If you are especially good shepherds, you can take care of my flocks, too." Then Joseph presented his father to the king. Pharaoh welcomed him kindly, and Jacob gave Pharaoh a special blessing.

So that is how Jacob's family got settled in Egypt.

DAY 50

A Blessing for Each Son

Genesis 48–50

Jacob lived in Egypt for seventeen years. Then he became very ill. Joseph took his two sons, Manasseh and Ephraim, to see their grandfather. Jacob blessed his grandsons.

68

He surprised Joseph by saying that the younger boy would be greater than the older one.

Then Jacob called all of his sons to come and receive his blessing: Leah's sons – Reuben, Simeon, Levi, Judah, Issachar, and Zebulun; Bilhah the slave-wife's sons – Dan and Naphtali; Zilpah the slave-wife's sons – Gad and Asher; Rachel's sons – Joseph and Benjamin.

Finally Jacob asked his sons to bury him in the family burial cave in Canaan. Then he lay down and died. Joseph was very sad. Pharaoh gave him permission to take Jacob's body to Canaan.

Joseph's brothers thought Joseph might turn against them now that Jacob was no longer alive. But Joseph said, "You thought you were harming me when I was a boy, but God turned that harm into good for all of us."

Joseph lived in Egypt all the rest of his life. When he died, he asked that his bones be taken back to Canaan. Four hundred years went by before that happened.

DAY 51
The Cruel Egyptians

Exodus 1

After Jacob and Joseph had both died, their families kept growing. Many years went by, and their children, grandchildren, and great-grandchildren were so many that it was almost impossible to count them. That is what God had said would happen when he had promised Abraham that his descendants would become a great nation.

After several hundred years, a pharaoh was ruling who didn't know anything about Joseph. This new pharaoh was worried about what a large nation the people of Israel had become. He thought they might become so powerful that they would turn against Egypt and help Egypt's enemies.

He also worried that they might decide to return to where they had come from and he would not have them to work for him anymore. So he ordered all the Egyptians to make the Israelites their slaves.

The Egyptians treated the people of Israel cruelly and made them work very hard. Because the Israelites were slaves, they were prisoners in Egypt. But God had promised to take care of them, and he always keeps his promises. More Israelite children were born, and the nation continued to grow.

70

The Baby in the Floating Basket

Exodus 1–2

When Pharaoh saw how the Israelite families were growing, he ordered the midwives, who helped the Israelite mothers when they were giving birth, to kill the baby boys as soon as they were born. The midwives knew this was wrong, so they disobeyed Pharaoh, and God blessed them because of it. Then Pharaoh told his own people to take the baby boys away from the Israelites and throw them into the Nile River.

A man and his wife, of the family of Levi, had a baby boy – their third child. They loved their little son, so they hid him, hoping no Egyptian would find him and kill him. When the baby was three months old, he was getting too big to hide.

His mother decided to weave a basket and make it waterproof by coating it with tar. Then she put her baby boy into the basket and hid it among the tall grasses at the edge of the river. The baby's older sister, Miriam, hid nearby to watch the basket and see what would happen to her baby brother.

A Princess Finds a Surprise

Exodus 2

Pharaoh had a daughter who went to bathe in the Nile River. As she was walking along the riverbank, the princess noticed the basket floating among the reeds. She sent one of her maids to pick it up out of the water and bring it to her.

When she looked inside, she was amazed to see a beautiful baby boy! The baby began to cry. The princess felt sorry for him and wanted to keep him safe. "I'm going to adopt this baby as my own," she said.

Just then Miriam, the baby's sister, came out from her hiding place. She asked the princess, "Would you like me to get one of the Jewish women to nurse him while he is so small?"

Pharaoh's daughter said, "Yes, please." So Miriam went home and got her mother. The princess said, "Take this baby home, and nurse him for me. I'll pay you for taking care of him."

So the baby's mother took care of her own little boy until he was old enough to go to live with the princess and be her adopted son. The princess named the little boy Moses.

DAY 54
Moses Escapes

Exodus 2

Although Moses grew up in the royal family, he never forgot that he was one of the people of Israel. One day he saw an Egyptian hitting one of his Israelite relatives. This made Moses terribly angry. He made sure no one was watching; then he killed the Egyptian and buried his body in the sand.

The next day he saw two Israelite men fighting. He said to the one who was in the wrong, "Why are you hitting your own Israelite brother?"

The man answered him angrily, "That's none of your business! You're not my judge. Do you plan to kill me the way you killed that Egyptian yesterday?"

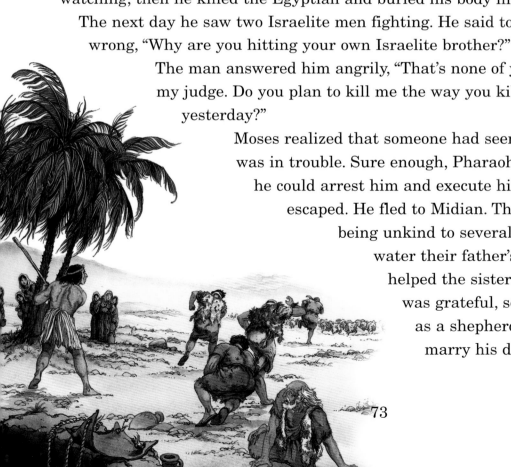

Moses realized that someone had seen his crime and that he was in trouble. Sure enough, Pharaoh tried to find Moses so he could arrest him and execute him for murder. But Moses escaped. He fled to Midian. There he saw some men being unkind to several sisters who wanted to water their father's sheep at a well. Moses helped the sisters. Their father, Reuel, was grateful, so he hired Moses to work as a shepherd and later let Moses marry his daughter Zipporah.

The Bush That Kept Burning

Exodus 3

While Moses was in Midian, the people of Israel were suffering in Egypt. They cried out to God for help, and he heard them. It was time to rescue his people. One day Moses was out tending his father-in-law's sheep. Suddenly he noticed something strange. A bush was on fire, but it wasn't burning up. He went closer. Then he heard a voice speaking to him.

"Moses!" the voice said. "I am God. Don't come any closer. Take off your shoes because this is holy ground." Moses was afraid to look at God, so he covered his face.

"I have heard my people in Egypt crying for help," God said. "I have chosen you to go to Pharaoh and tell him to let my people go. You are to lead them back to the land of promise."

"No!" Moses replied. "I could never do that."

"You can do it because I will be with you," God said.

Moses said, "If I tell the people you have sent me, they will ask, 'What is the name of this God?' What shall I say?"

God answered, "Tell them that 'I AM' has sent you."

Moses Can Do Miracles

Exodus 4

Although God promised Moses he would help him, Moses was still afraid. He thought the people wouldn't believe that God had talked to him. And Pharaoh would not want to let the slave-nation of Israel leave Egypt.

Finally God showed Moses how powerful he was. God told Moses to throw his shepherd's rod down on the ground. Moses obeyed, and immediately the rod turned into a live snake. Moses jumped away from it. Then God said to him, "Grab the snake by the tail."

Carefully Moses picked up the snake. Immediately it turned into a rod again. God said, "When you do that miracle, the people will believe I sent you. Now put your hand inside your robe, next to your chest."

When Moses did this and took his hand out again, it was covered with the disease leprosy.

"Do it again," God ordered. Moses did, and this time the leprosy was gone and his skin was healthy. "If the people don't believe the first miracle, they may believe the second – then they will listen to you."

Aaron Will Help His Brother

Exodus 4

God told Moses another way that he could prove he was God's messenger. He could take some water from the Nile River and pour it on the ground, and it would turn into blood. But Moses was still afraid and made another excuse. He said, "O Lord, I'm not a powerful speaker."

God said, "I can make you a good speaker, if you will only trust me." But Moses still didn't want to go. He said, "No, Lord. Find someone else to do this job."

God became angry with him. He said, "All right, I'll send your brother, Aaron, with you. He can speak for you. You tell him what to say, and he will deliver the messages. But I am going to give you the ability to talk well, too. Now take your shepherd's rod and go!"

Moses got his father-in-law's permission to leave. He took his wife and sons and started the trip. Before he left, God said, "The Pharaoh who wanted to kill you has died. Don't be afraid to go because no one in Egypt wants to hurt you anymore."

Pharaoh's Hard Heart

Exodus 4–5

God told Aaron to meet Moses at Mount Horeb. Moses told Aaron what God wanted them to do, and about the miraculous signs. They gave God's message to the leaders of the people of Israel, and Moses showed them the wonderful miracles. The elders of Israel believed that God had sent Moses and Aaron. They were very thankful that God had not forgotten them, and they worshipped the Lord.

Then Moses and Aaron went to tell Pharaoh what God had said. They said, "The Lord God of Israel has sent us to you with this message: 'Let my people go out into the desert to worship me.'"

Pharaoh was unimpressed. He said, "Who is this God, and why should I pay any attention to him? I refuse to let the Israelites stop work to make a trip. Now get out!" Then he ordered the supervisors to make the slaves work harder than ever. He said, "Don't give them any more straw. They must make as many bricks as before, but they must find their own straw. They'll be so busy they won't have time to think about trips to the desert!"

The People Complain to Moses

Exodus 5–7

The Israelite slaves suffered greatly as they had to work harder and harder. If they slowed down, the masters beat them and said they were lazy. The slaves blamed Moses and Aaron. "Everything is much worse for us since you asked Pharaoh to let us go," they said angrily. "You've made Pharaoh hate us. If he kills us, it will be your fault!"

Moses talked to God about this. "I thought you were going to rescue your people," he said. "But they are in worse trouble than before."

The Lord told Moses to be patient. He would see how well God would take care of the Israelites. God said, "Tell the people not to give up hope." Then he said they should try again with Pharaoh.

So Moses went back to Pharaoh and again asked him to release the slaves. This time Aaron threw down his rod and it became a snake. But Pharaoh's magicians were able to do the same miracle.

Then something exciting happened: Aaron's snake swallowed up all the magicians' snakes! Still Pharaoh was too stubborn to let the slaves go.

Big Trouble for Egypt

Exodus 7–8

Again God told Moses to speak to Pharaoh, so Moses met Pharaoh the next morning by the river. Moses repeated his message from God, but Pharaoh said no. Then the Lord told Aaron to point his rod over the river. Aaron did this and then struck the water. At that very moment all the water in the river – and all the other water in Egypt – changed into blood.

The fish all died, and the people of Egypt had no clean water to drink. This went on for seven days, but Pharaoh still refused to let the people go.

The next week Aaron pointed his rod again, and thousands of frogs appeared. They filled the whole country. They were everywhere! Pharaoh begged Moses and Aaron to get rid of the frogs. "If you do," he said, "I will let the people go to the desert."

"When shall I do this?" Moses asked.

"Tomorrow," Pharaoh answered.

So the next day all the frogs died. But Pharaoh changed his mind and broke his promise to Moses.

Pharaoh begged
Moses and Aaron to
get rid of the frogs.

80

Frightening Punishments

Exodus 8–10

God kept giving Pharaoh chances to let the people go. Each time, Pharaoh said he would; then at the last moment he would break his word. God made the dust turn into insects called gnats, which made life miserable. Then swarms of flies came down upon the Egyptians. The next punishment was a disease that killed the animals.

Then awful sores called boils broke out all over people's skin. Next God sent a violent storm that destroyed the crops and hurt the Egyptians.

Pharaoh tried to make a deal with Moses to let only the men go but Moses wouldn't agree. This time God sent a great swarm of locusts that ate up every plant, tree, and blade of grass. Pharaoh said he would let the people go if Moses got rid of the locusts. But he didn't keep that promise either.

Next God sent a thick darkness over Egypt. For three days people were afraid to move because they couldn't see a thing. Pharaoh said, "Take the people, but leave the animals behind." But Moses said that wasn't what God had told them to do. So again Pharaoh refused to let them go.

81

The Worst Punishment

Exodus 11

Finally God said to Moses, "I'm going to send one final, dreadful punishment. When it is over, Pharaoh will beg you to take my people and go. But first, tell my people to ask their Egyptian friends and neighbours to give them pieces of gold and silver jewellery."

So Moses went to Pharaoh one more time and said, "God is going to come in the middle of the night, and the first-born son in every home will die. Your own son will die, Pharaoh, along with all the other first-born. Every Egyptian family will be in deep sorrow. But no Israelite child shall die. The Israelites are very special to God, and he will take care of them. You will beg us to leave the country. Then I will take my people and go."

Moses turned and hurried out of the palace. He already knew that Pharaoh would not listen to him. God had hardened the king's heart so he could show everyone his own power and glory.

The First Passover

Exodus 12

Moses and Aaron's next job was to tell the people of Israel what God wanted them to do. They had to get ready for the night when God would visit the homes of the Egyptians and kill the firstborn sons. Here are the instructions God gave them:

1. Each family should kill a perfect one-year-old lamb or baby goat.
2. They should use a certain weed as a brush and paint some of the lamb's blood on each side and over the top of their front door.
3. Then they should roast the lamb and eat it, along with the bitter-tasting herbs and hard bread made without yeast.
4. They must eat all of it that night and not save any for the next day.

5. While they eat it, they are to wear their travelling clothes and their sandals and carry a walking stick.

Then God made a wonderful promise to his people. He said "When I go through the land killing the firstborn of the Egyptians, I will see the blood on your doors. That will show me that you have obeyed my instructions, and I will pass over your homes and not kill your firstborn sons." He said that from then on, they were to have this ceremony on a certain day every year in memory of his goodness to them. The annual celebration should be called "the Lord's Passover", because he had passed over their homes when he saw the blood on the doors.

DAY 64

Pharaoh Lets the People Go

Exodus 12

The people of Israel followed God's instructions. At midnight the Lord passed through the nation of Egypt, and the first-born in every family died. Even the firstborn cattle died. All the Egyptian people got up in the middle of the night to see what had happened. They were all heartbroken to find that in every Egyptian home someone had died.

Pharaoh knew this tragedy had happened because he had not listened to the warnings of Moses and Aaron. Quickly he called them to his court and said, "Hurry and leave my country! Take your families and your flocks and herds of animals. Get out quickly, and worship your God any way you want to. But before you go, please bless me." The Israelites asked their Egyptian friends and neighbours for gold and silver jewellery, and the Egyptians gladly gave it to them. Then the people of Israel packed up all their things and set out – 600,000 men, plus all the women and children.

They became angry with Moses and said, "It's all your fault. You took us away from Egypt and brought us to this desert place. Now we are all going to die without water."

Moses asked God what he should do. God told Moses to take the people to Mount Horeb. "Go to the rock I will show you. Then take your rod and hit the rock. Immediately, water will pour out." Moses did exactly what God told him to do, and water flowed from the rock. There was plenty for all the people to drink.

DAY 69

Joshua Leads the Army

Exodus 17

While the people were still at Rephidim, an army from Amalek attacked them. Moses chose a very brave man named Joshua to lead Israel's army. He said, "Joshua, choose the men you need, and go and fight the Amalekites. I will stand on a hill and watch. Aaron and Hur will be with me. I'll hold up my rod and point it out over the army. As long as I hold it there, God will give you and your soldiers victory."

While Moses held the rod up, the people of Israel defeated the Amalekites. But sometimes his arms got so tired that he had to lower the rod. Then the Amalekites started to win the battle.

Aaron and Hur got a big rock for Moses to sit on. They stood, one on each side of Moses, and held up his arms so that the rod was always pointing out over the battlefield. Finally the battle was over, and the Israelite army had won.

God told Moses he would one day destroy all the people of Amalek. Then Moses built an altar and named it "The Lord Is My Battle Flag".

DAY 70
God Calls Moses to the Mountain

Exodus 19

After the war with the Amalekites, the people of Israel continued to travel. They camped at Mount Sinai, where God told Moses to climb the mountain to talk with him. God said, "Tell the people how much I love them. I have rescued them from Egypt and have taken care of them. They will always be my special servants – a holy nation."

Moses gave the people God's message. They promised to obey God and be his special people. Then God told Moses that the people must prepare themselves for a time when God would send them important instructions and rules. They must get their hearts ready to hear what God would tell them. They would hear a trumpet call, and they would know that God was ready to speak to them through Moses. Only Moses was allowed to go up onto the mountain.

The trumpet sounded, and smoke rose from the mountain. All the people stood around the foot of it while Moses climbed up to meet God.

Commandments about Loving God

Exodus 20

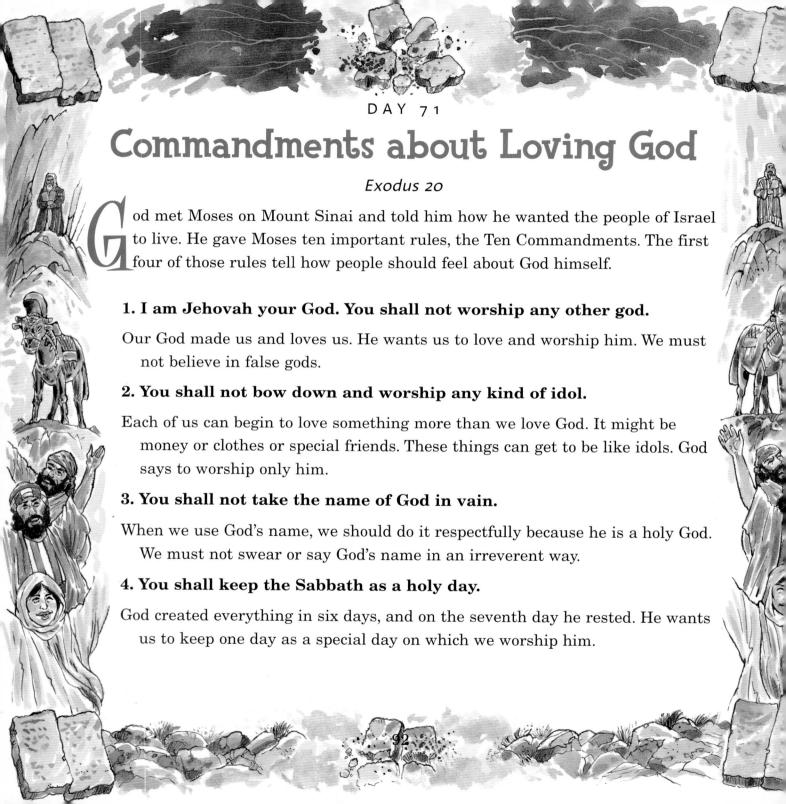

God met Moses on Mount Sinai and told him how he wanted the people of Israel to live. He gave Moses ten important rules, the Ten Commandments. The first four of those rules tell how people should feel about God himself.

1. I am Jehovah your God. You shall not worship any other god.

Our God made us and loves us. He wants us to love and worship him. We must not believe in false gods.

2. You shall not bow down and worship any kind of idol.

Each of us can begin to love something more than we love God. It might be money or clothes or special friends. These things can get to be like idols. God says to worship only him.

3. You shall not take the name of God in vain.

When we use God's name, we should do it respectfully because he is a holy God. We must not swear or say God's name in an irreverent way.

4. You shall keep the Sabbath as a holy day.

God created everything in six days, and on the seventh day he rested. He wants us to keep one day as a special day on which we worship him.

Commandments about Loving Others

Exodus 20

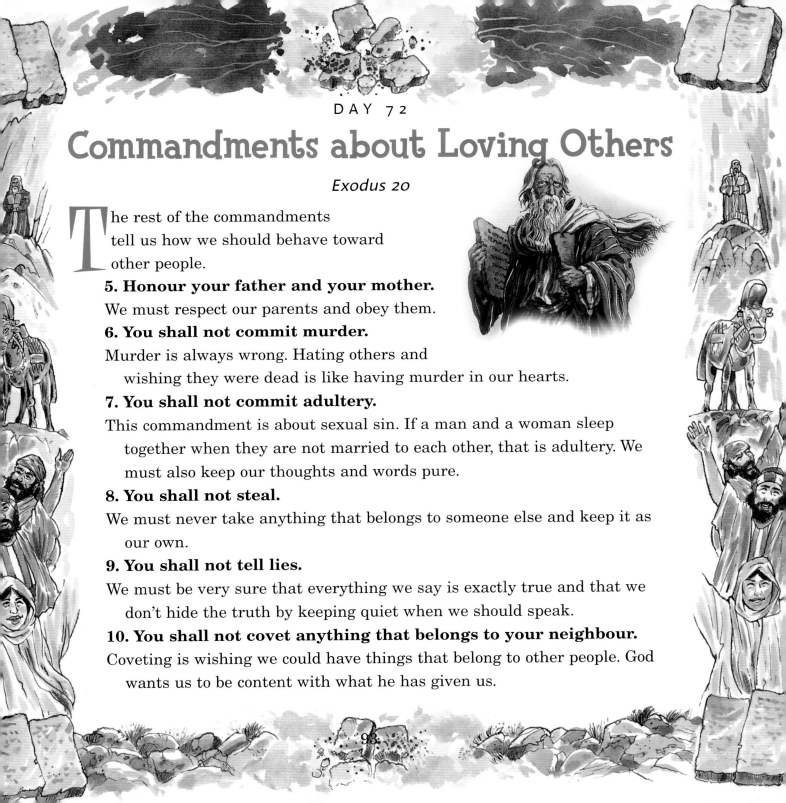

The rest of the commandments tell us how we should behave toward other people.

5. Honour your father and your mother.

We must respect our parents and obey them.

6. You shall not commit murder.

Murder is always wrong. Hating others and wishing they were dead is like having murder in our hearts.

7. You shall not commit adultery.

This commandment is about sexual sin. If a man and a woman sleep together when they are not married to each other, that is adultery. We must also keep our thoughts and words pure.

8. You shall not steal.

We must never take anything that belongs to someone else and keep it as our own.

9. You shall not tell lies.

We must be very sure that everything we say is exactly true and that we don't hide the truth by keeping quiet when we should speak.

10. You shall not covet anything that belongs to your neighbour.

Coveting is wishing we could have things that belong to other people. God wants us to be content with what he has given us.

A Special House for God

Exodus 24–27

The people promised to obey God's rules. Then God called Moses back to the mountain so he could give him the Ten Commandments carved on pieces of stone. Moses took Joshua with him. God told Moses he wanted the people to build a special place in which to worship him. He described it to Moses very carefully. Because the people were travelling, it had to be easy to move, so God said it must be a tent that could be carried. This building was to be called the Tabernacle.

Then God described the furniture that should go into the Tabernacle. One of the most important pieces would be the Ark of the Covenant, a beautiful chest made of wood and then covered with gold. The cover of the Ark would be called the mercy seat. They were also to make a table, a lampstand with seven lamps, and altars on which offerings would be made and incense burned.

God told Moses to ask the people to provide the different materials as a gift to God. Moses would need gold, silver, bronze, beautiful cloth, wood, oil, spices, incense, and jewels.

Clothes for the Priests

Exodus 28

God appointed Aaron and his family to be in charge of the worship that would take place in the Tabernacle. Aaron would be the High Priest, and his four sons would help him. It would be the priests' job to sacrifice the animals the people brought as offerings to God.

God wanted the priests to have special clothing to show that they had been especially chosen for their work. Aaron would wear an embroidered robe covered by a blue coat. Around the hem of the coat would be bells and decorations in the shape of pomegranates. Over the coat he was to wear a cloth vest, called an ephod, which had twelve kinds of jewels sewn onto the front. Each jewel represented one of the tribes of Israel.

Aaron was to wear special shirts and undergarments. On his head he should wear a linen turban with a gold plate on the front of it, with the words Holiness to the Lord. Aaron's sons were also to wear robes, sashes, and turbans. God told Moses to have a special dedication ceremony for the priests.

Dedicating the Priests

Exodus 29

God gave Moses more details about the dedication of Aaron and his sons. He was to prepare special bread and bring a young bull and two rams that were perfect. He was to have Aaron and his sons bathe at the entrance to the Tabernacle, then dress them in the clothing God had described. He should pour oil on Aaron's head. This showed that a person was chosen to do a very special work for God.

Next they should offer first the young bull and then the rams to God. The meat and the bread were symbols, or signs, of obedience, setting Aaron and his sons apart from all the other people. They were priests in the house of God – the Tabernacle.

This ceremony was to be repeated every day for seven days. As offerings were made on the altar, the altar was dedicated to God and became a holy place of offering and worship. God said that if these instructions were followed carefully, he would always live among the people of Israel and be the Lord their God.

Important Rules to Obey

Leviticus 17–22

God wanted his people to be like himself. Like him, they were to be fair, kind, loving, pure, and holy. God gave them instructions about getting along with other people and keeping their hearts and their actions pure.

He taught them to leave some of their grain and grapes in the fields for poor people. He said they should never steal nor tell lies. If they owed other people money, they should pay it as soon as possible. They should be loving and kind, to each other and to foreigners who might live nearby. They must never take advantage of handicapped people.

God said, "You must never copy what your ungodly neighbours do, worshipping false gods by sacrificing their children and having the wrong kinds of sexual relationships with others." He made it very clear that his people were to be different from other people in the world because they were his chosen ones – chosen to show God's character and his glory. So he set very high standards for them and expected them to obey him perfectly.

Special Holidays

Leviticus 23–24

God told the people of Israel to observe special holidays. One of these was the Sabbath, the day on which they rested and worshipped God, remembering how God rested after creating the world and everything in it.

Three of their most important holidays were:

1. **The Passover**. This reminded them of how God passed over the homes of his people when he killed the firstborn children of the Egyptians and helped his people escape from Egypt.

2. **The Harvest Festival**. This was a day of thanksgiving after all the crops had been gathered. The people were to praise God for sending the rain and sunshine.

3. **The Tabernacle Festival**. This reminded the people of the way they lived as they travelled from Egypt to Canaan, the Promised Land. For a whole week they were to move out of their regular houses and live in huts formed from tree branches woven together. At each of these celebrations, the people were to bring gifts to God – olive oil for the lamps in the Tabernacle and fresh bread to put on the gold table.

DAY 86

A Big Celebration

Leviticus 25

Every seven years the people of Israel had a Sabbath year, when they rested and didn't plant any crops. After seven of those Sabbath years, God gave them a year of special celebration on the fiftieth year. It was called the Year of Jubilee. During that year the people didn't grow crops but had plenty to eat because they had saved food from the year before. Also, if they had had to sell any of their land to pay their debts, on the Year of Jubilee they would get their land back, reminding them that the land really belonged to God and was theirs only as his gift.

The Israelites were told to be especially kind to each other and to foreigners among them during that year. God said, "If any of your fellow Israelites have become your slaves because they owed you money, you must let them go free." All the people were very glad when it was time for a Year of Jubilee because so many good things happened to them during that year!

The Levites Work in the Tabernacle

Numbers 1–4

More than a year after they had left Egypt, the people of Israel moved on from Mount Sinai. Moses and Aaron counted over six thousand men who could be soldiers. They came from every tribe except the Levites. The Levites had the special job of looking after the Tabernacle and were not to fight in wars.

When it was time to move, the Levites had to take the Tabernacle apart and carry it as they were travelling. Most of the Tabernacle was carried in wagons, but the Ark, the lampstand, and the gold and bronze altars had to be carried on the shoulders of Levites. When the cloud stopped and the people stopped to make camp, the Levites put the Tabernacle together again.

The Levites were also the ones who made all the sacrifices when the people brought animals as their offerings to God. They carried wood to burn and water for washing, and then they had to carry the ashes away from the altars after the sacrifices were burned.

It was a great privilege to be a Levite and work in the Tabernacle.

DAY 92
The Earth Swallows Korah

Numbers 16

As if the people hadn't complained enough about Moses, Korah and three of his friends stirred up more trouble by persuading 250 important leaders to join them in a rebellion against Moses and Aaron. They said to Moses, "We are tired of your ordering us around. You are no better than the rest of us. Why should Aaron get to be High Priest?" Moses prayed; then he answered them, "We'll find out whether God has really chosen us. Come back tomorrow with fire in your incense burners, and we'll see what God has to say."

The next day they were back with their censers. The people of Israel gathered around Korah and the other rebels. Then Moses spoke to Korah: "Aren't you satisfied to be a worker in God's house of worship? Must you try to take the place of God's appointed servant?"

Then Moses warned everyone to get away from Korah and the rebels. He said, "God will show you who should be your leaders." As soon as he had finished speaking, the earth opened and swallowed up Korah and his rebellious friends.

DAY 93
Buds, Blossoms, and Fruit

Numbers 16–17

The people of Israel were afraid when Korah and the rebels were punished by God. They ran away so they wouldn't be killed too. As they thought about what had happened to Korah, they became angry and started criticising Moses and

Aaron again. While they were grumbling, they suddenly saw the cloud over the Tabernacle. This showed that God was present.

Then God spoke, saying, "I'm going to destroy these stubborn people."

Moses and Aaron prayed for them, but almost fifteen thousand people died.

God said, "Now I'll stop all this grumbling against my chosen leaders. Moses, tell the chief of each tribe to carve his name on a wooden rod. The rod from the tribe of Levi should have Aaron's name on it. Put the rods in front of the Ark in the Tabernacle. The true leader's rod will sprout buds."

Moses followed God's instructions. The next day Aaron's rod had not only buds on it but blossoms and ripe almonds too! From that time on, Aaron's rod was always kept in the Tabernacle. Whenever anyone complained, Moses showed him the rod.

DAY 94

Moses Loses His Temper

Numbers 20

The people moved on to the Zin Desert, where Moses' sister, Miriam, died. When they ran out of water, they blamed Moses! "Why didn't you just kill us along with Korah?" God told Moses and Aaron to take Aaron's rod and stand in front of a certain rock. "Speak to that rock, and water will gush out."

Moses went to the rock, but then he lost his temper. He shouted, "You stubborn rebels! Must I always get water for you?" Then he hit the rock twice with the rod. Immediately water gushed out, and everyone had plenty to drink.

But God said, "You didn't obey me. Because you struck the rock instead of speaking to it, you and Aaron may not enter the Promised Land."

Soon the Lord told Moses it was time for Aaron to die. He said, "Take Aaron and his son Eleazar up onto Mount Hor." Then God told Moses to remove Aaron's priestly clothing and put it on Eleazar. As Moses did this, Aaron died. Moses and Eleazar descended from the mountain to join the people who were waiting at the bottom.

"God has appointed Eleazar to take Aaron's place," Moses told the people.

Bitten by Poisonous Snakes

Numbers 21

The people had been travelling for almost forty years, and everyone was getting tired and discouraged. Once again they grumbled at Moses. "We don't have enough water and food, and we are tired of eating manna."

Their ungrateful attitude angered God, so he punished them by sending poisonous snakes into the camp to bite them. Many died. The people were sorry that they had complained, so they cried to Moses, "Please pray that God will take the snakes away and save our lives."

Moses asked the Lord to help his people. God said, "Make a snake out of bronze, and fasten it to the top of a long pole. Raise it high over the camp where people can look up

115

at it. Everyone who does so will be healed of snakebite and will not die." Moses did this, and many lives were spared.

Moses needed permission for the Israelites to travel through some land belonging to King Sihon, a powerful Amorite king. King Sihon refused and attacked the Israelites at Jahaz. But the Israelites won and were able to travel throughout the land of the Amorites.

DAY 96

The Talking Donkey

Numbers 22

When the Israelites came near the plains of Moab, King Balak became frightened. He had heard what they had done to the armies of the Amorites! He sent messengers to offer money to Balaam if he would curse Israel.

Balaam wanted the money, so he saddled his donkey and followed the king's messengers. But God didn't want anyone to curse his special people, so he sent an angel to stop Balaam. The angel stood in front of Balaam with a sword in his hand. Balaam couldn't see the angel, but his donkey could. The donkey turned away and left the road. Balaam didn't understand, so he beat the donkey.

Further along the road, the donkey saw the angel again. There was a wall on either side, and, frightened, she pressed up against it, crushing Balaam's foot. This made him angry, so he beat her again.

On the third occasion, the donkey collapsed under Balaam. Again he beat her. This time an amazing thing happened; the donkey spoke, asking, "Why have you beaten me three times?"

Then the Lord let Balaam see the angel, and Balaam was sorry he had treated the donkey so badly. The angel told him to go and see King Balak but say only what God told him.

DAY 97
Curses Turn to Blessings

Numbers 23–25

Balaam went on with Balak's messengers, and the king came out to meet him. "At last you are here," he said. "Yes," said Balaam, "but I'll speak only what God puts in my mouth." The next day Balaam told Balak to build seven altars and prepare seven bulls and seven rams for sacrifice. He and King Balak each sacrificed a bull and a ram. Then Balaam asked God what to say about Israel. God told him, and when Balaam spoke, everything he said was a blessing upon the people of Israel.

This made Balak really angry. He took Balaam to a different place, and they built seven more altars and made sacrifices. Again Balaam asked God's advice, and again he was allowed to speak only good things.

Balak said, "Maybe you can't curse my enemies, but don't bless them!" The same thing happened again, and so Balak said, "Go home, but don't expect any pay."

Balak thought of another way to bring trouble upon Israel. He threw a party to honour Canaanite idols. He invited some young Israelites, and soon they started to worship the false gods along with the Canaanites. As Balak had expected, God became angry, and he sent a disease that killed thousands of his people.

The View Across the River

Numbers 25–26

The forty years of wandering were almost over. Before God could let the people go into the Promised Land, he had to be sure all of the older generation had died, so he asked Moses to count the people. Caleb and Joshua had been faithful, trusting spies and were the only older people allowed to go into Canaan. Because the people of Midian had led many of the Israelites into idol worship, God said his people must make war on Midian. So they killed all the Midianites and kept their animals and burned down all their cities.

After the war, God's people were grateful because not one of the Israelite soldiers had been killed. To show their gratitude, they offered to Moses and Eleazar all the jewellery they had taken from the Midianites. Moses and Eleazar accepted the jewellery and put it in the Tabernacle as a thank-offering to God.

At last the people of Israel stood on the banks of the Jordan River. They looked across it into the Promised Land and thanked the Lord that it was almost time to enter Canaan.

The People Are Divided

Numbers 32

The tribes of Reuben, Gad, and the half-tribe of Manasseh were camped beside the Jordan River. They asked Moses if they could make their permanent home there instead of on the opposite side of the river, where the other tribes would be settling.

Moses got angry with them. "What's the matter? Are you so afraid of the people in Canaan that you want to avoid a war with them? Do you want the other tribes to do your fighting for you?"

"No, not at all," they replied. "But the land on this side of the river looks like a wonderful place for our flocks and herds, because there's plenty of pastureland. We want to leave our families and animals here and come across the river with everyone else. We'll fight until the Canaanites are destroyed. Then we can come back here and settle down with our families."

Moses thought it over. He asked everyone else who was camped by the river what they thought. Everyone agreed to let them have the land they wanted, if they helped to wipe out the Canaanite enemies first.

DAY 100
Safe from Revenge

Numbers 35

Moses made plans for when his people would be living in Canaan, the Promised Land, without him because of his earlier disobedience. He told them that certain cities were to be given to the Levites for their special use. Each of those cities would have plenty of pastureland around it for their flocks.

Other special cities were to be called cities of refuge, or cities of safety. Those cities were places where someone could run for safety if he had accidentally killed someone. A relative of the dead person might try to get revenge on the killer. But once a killer was inside a city of safety and had told his story to the judges there, no one could harm him. The killer had to stay in the city of safety until after the death of the high priest. Then he could go back home, and no one could punish him for the accidental killing. The cities of safety were not intended to protect murderers but only those who had not meant to cause another person's death.

DAY 101
Moses' Long Speech

Deuteronomy 32–34

Since Moses wasn't going into Canaan, he made a long speech, reminding his people of everything that had happened since they left Egypt. He didn't want them to forget God's goodness during the past forty years.

Moses had seen how easily the people forgot God's instructions and how often they disobeyed God. He reminded them of all the commandments that told them how God wanted them to live. He said, "Don't forget: You must never worship any other God.

Don't make idols or worship them. Don't use God's name carelessly, and always keep the Sabbath day holy. Honour your father and mother. You must never murder or commit adultery or steal or lie. And you must not desire anything that belongs to someone else." Then he reminded them about the other 613 rules. And he repeated what they had learned about the feasts and festivals they were to observe, each one a reminder of the good things God had done for them.

Finally he told them that Joshua was to be their new leader.

Then he climbed to the top of Mount Nebo and looked across the river at the Promised Land. And there Moses died at the age of 120.

DAY 102

Joshua Becomes the Leader

Joshua 1

After Moses died, Joshua became the leader of the people of Israel. He had been Moses' assistant and one of the two faithful spies who had brought back a good report from Canaan and had encouraged the people to trust God for safety.

God said to Joshua, "Get the people ready to cross the Jordan River. I will give you all the land you walk on. Don't be afraid to go into Canaan. I will be with you and will take care of you. Just obey me and be brave."

Joshua told the people to get ready to cross the river. He reminded the tribes of Reuben, Gad, and the half-tribe of Manasseh that their wives and children could stay on the east side of the river, but they must go across and help the other tribes get rid of the hostile Canaanites, as God had directed them. Later, when the wars were over, they could rejoin their families and go on being herdsmen on their fertile plots of land. Everyone promised to obey and follow Joshua because God had chosen him to be the leader.

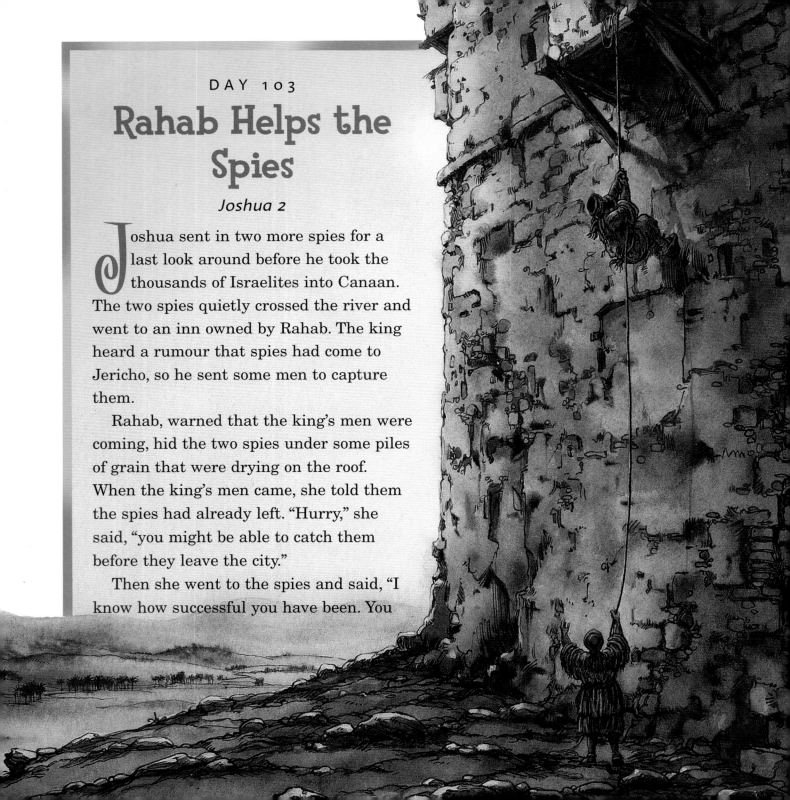

Rahab Helps the Spies

Joshua 2

Joshua sent in two more spies for a last look around before he took the thousands of Israelites into Canaan. The two spies quietly crossed the river and went to an inn owned by Rahab. The king heard a rumour that spies had come to Jericho, so he sent some men to capture them.

Rahab, warned that the king's men were coming, hid the two spies under some piles of grain that were drying on the roof. When the king's men came, she told them the spies had already left. "Hurry," she said, "you might be able to catch them before they leave the city."

Then she went to the spies and said, "I know how successful you have been. You must worship a very powerful God. I know that your God will give you the victory over Jericho. I want you to save me and my family because we have helped you today." The spies told Rahab to hang a red rope in the window of her home and stay inside with her family. When the people of Israel captured the city, they would see the rope and know that it was Rahab's home.

Crossing the River

Joshua 3–4

The spies returned to the camp, and the people gathered by the Jordan River, ready to cross. The next morning the priests appointed to carry the Ark went first. As they stepped into the water, the river stopped flowing, and the priests walked into the middle of it. While they held up the Ark, everyone else crossed safely over.

God told Joshua, "Choose twelve men, one from each tribe, to pick up twelve large stones from the middle of the riverbed and carry them to the far bank. The priests should stay in the middle of the riverbed."

When everyone was safely on the other side, the priests continued to cross the riverbed. As soon as they stepped onto the bank, the water started to flow again! The people made a camp at a place called Gilgal. They used the twelve stones from the riverbed to build a monument. Joshua said, "One day your children and grandchildren will ask, 'What is that stone monument for?' You must tell them about this wonderful day when God opened up the waters of the Jordan River and let his people walk across on dry land. He did this to show everyone how powerful he is."

The Lord Visits Joshua

Joshua 5

The people of Israel were happy to be in Canaan. One of the first things they did was to celebrate the Passover, reminding them of the night when the Angel of the Lord passed over their homes.

In Gilgal they were glad to find some corn growing in the fields because they were tired of eating manna. Now that they were in a country where they could find food and could start growing crops, the manna soon stopped appearing on the ground.

Joshua knew that one of his biggest jobs would be to capture Jericho and occupy it. As he was thinking about how he and his army could successfully make war on Jericho, a man appeared to him, holding a sword in his hand. Joshua asked, "Are you for us or for our enemies?"

The man replied, "I have come as the commander in chief of the Lord's army."

Joshua knew that the man was really the Lord himself, so he fell down and worshipped him.

Then the commander said to him, as he had said to Moses at the burning bush, "Take off your shoes. You are standing on holy ground."

A City's Walls Fall Down

Joshua 6

The commander of the Lord's army told Joshua that God would give him the victory. He told him exactly how to win the battle. Joshua agreed to obey what the Lord told him to do.

Joshua's soldiers marched around the city wall with the priests who carried the Ark of the Covenant. Ahead of the Ark walked seven priests blowing trumpets. The army and the priests did this every day for six days.

On the seventh day everyone started marching earlier than usual because this time they had to march around the walls of Jericho seven times. As usual, the seven priests blew on their trumpets while they were marching. At the end of the seventh time, the priests gave a loud blast and Joshua ordered, "Shout aloud, for the Lord has given you victory over the city!" The soldiers shouted, and the walls fell down with a great crash!

The soldiers marched into Jericho and captured it, but they remembered to take care of Rahab and her family. Then the army burned the city down, but they put the valuable things into the Lord's treasury.

133

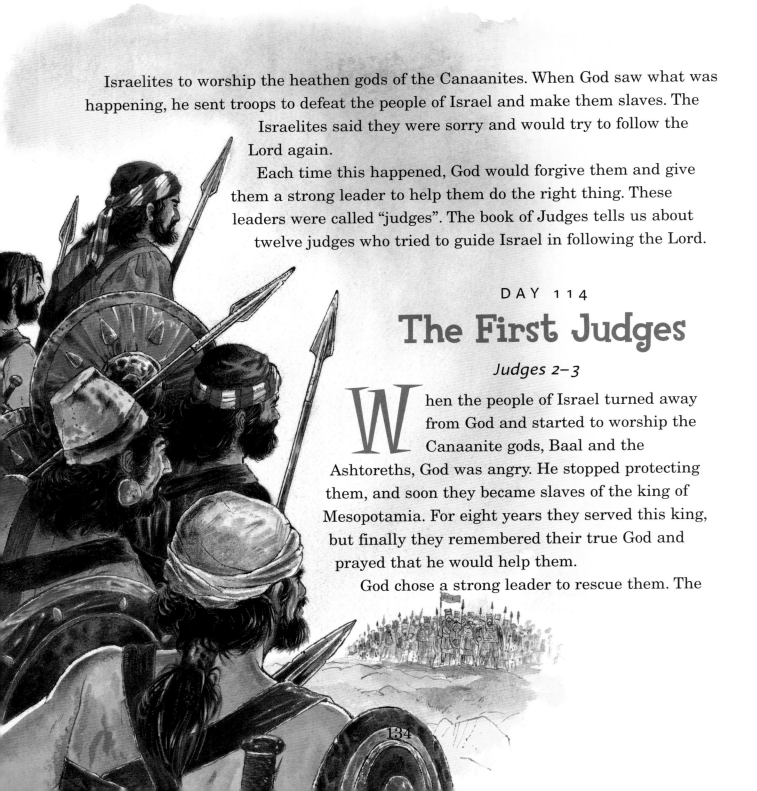

Israelites to worship the heathen gods of the Canaanites. When God saw what was happening, he sent troops to defeat the people of Israel and make them slaves. The Israelites said they were sorry and would try to follow the Lord again.

Each time this happened, God would forgive them and give them a strong leader to help them do the right thing. These leaders were called "judges". The book of Judges tells us about twelve judges who tried to guide Israel in following the Lord.

DAY 114

The First Judges

Judges 2–3

When the people of Israel turned away from God and started to worship the Canaanite gods, Baal and the Ashtoreths, God was angry. He stopped protecting them, and soon they became slaves of the king of Mesopotamia. For eight years they served this king, but finally they remembered their true God and prayed that he would help them.

God chose a strong leader to rescue them. The

leader, or judge, was Othniel. God sent his Spirit to Othniel, and Othniel saved the Israelites from the king of Mesopotamia. For forty years they obeyed God and had peace in the land.

When Othniel died, the people began to forget God again. They became subjects of a Moabite king named Eglon, and they had to pay heavy taxes to him. Then God sent Ehud, a Benjamite, to help them. Ehud went to see King Eglon and pretended he needed to talk to him alone. The king's aides left, and then Ehud stabbed Eglon. By the time the king's men found Eglon, Ehud had escaped. He led Israel in war against the Moabites. Israel won, and for eighty years they had peace.

The next judge was Shamgar, and he helped the Israelites get victory over the Philistines. But soon the people forgot God again.

DAY 115

Deborah Leads an Army

Judges 4

For about twenty years the Israelites had to serve King Jabin. The head of his army was a cruel man named Sisera. The people of Israel used to come to Deborah, a prophetess, and she would settle their problems with wise decisions.

Deborah sent for Barak and said, "God wants you to lead the fight against General Sisera. God will give you the victory." But Barak was afraid. "I can't go to war unless you go with me." Deborah said, "All right, but a woman will get the credit, not you." They gathered an army of ten thousand men and marched into battle.

God sent confusion and panic into the enemy forces, and Barak's troops destroyed every one of them – except Sisera, who fled. He escaped to the camp of some allies of King Jabin. A woman named Jael invited him to hide in her tent. She gave him a drink of milk and told him to rest. When Sisera was asleep, Jael killed him by hammering a sharp tent peg through his head.

When Barak came by, chasing Sisera, Jael showed him Sisera's body. Soon afterward Jabin and his people were completely destroyed.

DAY 116

God Chooses Gideon as Leader

Judges 6

After forty peaceful years, Israel again started to worship other gods. The Lord sent the Midianites against them, and for seven years the people suffered terribly. They cried to God for help, and he chose a leader named Gideon. Gideon was threshing grain secretly in a grape press when the Angel of the Lord appeared and said, "The Lord is with you, mighty warrior!"

Gideon replied bitterly, "If the Lord is with us, why has he left us to the mercy of Midian? Besides, I'm not a mighty warrior. I'm just a farm boy."

"God will use you to get your people out of trouble," the Lord answered.

"How can I be sure? Wait here,

and I'll bring you an offering." Gideon got meat, broth, and bread.

The Lord told him to put the bread and meat on a rock and pour the broth over it. The Lord touched it with his walking stick, and fire flamed up from the rock, burning up the offering. Immediately the Lord disappeared. Gideon was afraid he would die because he had seen the Lord, but the voice of the Lord said, "Don't worry. You won't die." Gideon built an altar there and called it "Peace with God".

137

Is the Wool Wet or Dry?

Judges 6

That night the Lord told Gideon to tear down his father's altar to Baal and break down the idols. "Then build an altar to the Lord and sacrifice a young bull. Use one of the idols as wood for the fire." Gideon was afraid, but he obeyed.

In the morning the village men were amazed at what they saw. When they found out Gideon had done it, they said, "He must die because of what he did to Baal's altar and the idols."

But Gideon's father said, "Why are you defending Baal? If he's a real god, he can take care of himself." So the men left Gideon alone.

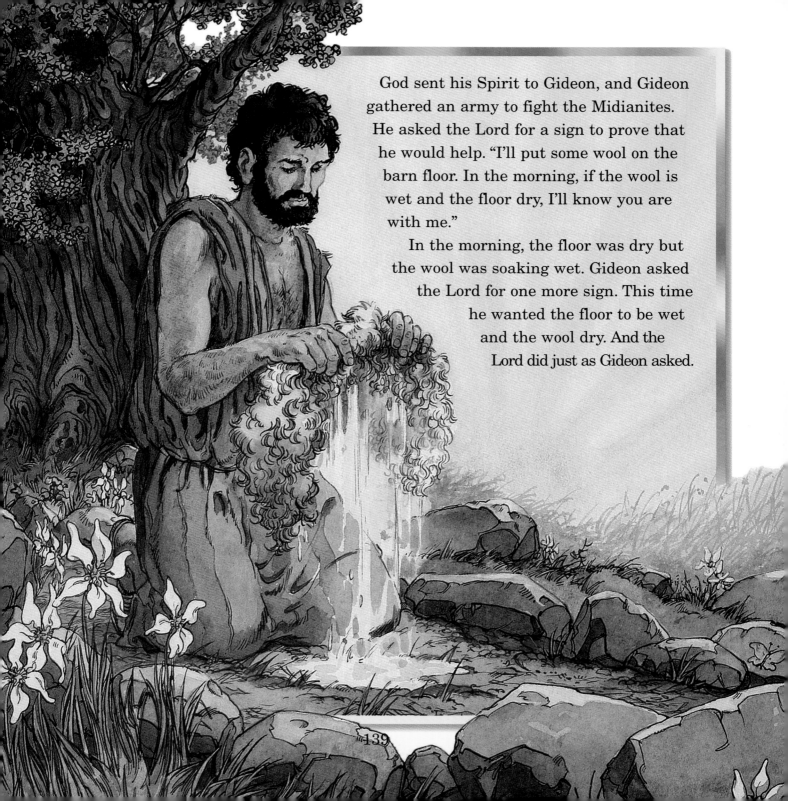

God sent his Spirit to Gideon, and Gideon gathered an army to fight the Midianites. He asked the Lord for a sign to prove that he would help. "I'll put some wool on the barn floor. In the morning, if the wool is wet and the floor dry, I'll know you are with me."

In the morning, the floor was dry but the wool was soaking wet. Gideon asked the Lord for one more sign. This time he wanted the floor to be wet and the wool dry. And the Lord did just as Gideon asked.

Gideon's Army Wins

Judges 7

Gideon gathered about thirty-two thousand men to fight the Midianites. The Lord said, "Send home all who are fearful about the battle." About twenty-two thousand of them went home. Then God said, "You still have too many. Take them down to the edge of the water, and let them drink water from the spring. Those who pick up water in their hands and lap it like dogs are the ones you should take into battle. Send home those who get down on their knees and drink from the spring."

Only three hundred soldiers drank from their hands. The Lord said, "I'll conquer the Midianites with these men."

Gideon gave each soldier a trumpet and a pitcher containing a lighted lamp. He said, "When we get close to the Midianites' camp, we will blow our trumpets, break our pitchers, and shout, 'The sword of the Lord and of Gideon!'" When they broke their pitchers and shouted, the Midianites were frightened. The noise and lights made them think there were more soldiers than there were.

Gideon's army defeated them and captured their two kings. At last Israel was free of the cruel Midianites.

Samson Kills a Lion

Judges 14

Samson's parents wanted him to marry an Israelite girl, but he insisted on marrying a Philistine woman. On the way to her home, a lion attacked Samson and his parents. God's Spirit gave Samson strength to kill the lion with his bare hands.

Sometime later Samson saw that bees had made a hive in the lion's carcass and that the carcass was full of honey.

Samson gave a wedding feast. He challenged thirty young men to a contest. "If you guess the answer to a riddle," he said, "I'll give you each some new clothes. If you cannot answer, you must each give me some clothes."

"What's the riddle?" they asked.

"Food came out of the eater and sweetness came out of the strong," Samson said.

Samson's bride cried until he told her the answer. At the end of the contest the young Philistine men answered, "What is sweeter than honey, and what is stronger than a lion?"

Samson realised that his bride had told them the answer. Her disloyalty made him angry, so Samson deserted his new wife and went back to Israel.

143

Samson Punishes His Enemies

Judges 15

After a while, Samson calmed down, so he went to see his wife. Her father said, "I thought you weren't coming back, so I let your best man marry her." Samson was furious. He caught three hundred foxes, tied their tails together, and fastened a burning torch to each pair. The foxes ran through the Philistines' fields, setting fire to all their crops.

When the Philistines found out why he had done this, they killed the girl and her father. That made Samson even angrier. He attacked and killed more Philistines. For a time he stayed in Judah. The Philistines chased Samson and asked the men of Judah to help them capture him. The men of Judah told Samson to stop upsetting the Philistines and wanted to turn him over to the Philistines themselves. Samson said, "Just don't kill me yourselves."

The men of Judah tied him up with some new ropes and took him to the Philistines. Then the Spirit of God made Samson very strong. He broke the ropes, grabbed the jawbone of a dead donkey, and used it to kill a thousand Philistines.

An Unfaithful Girlfriend

Judges 16

Samson had a girlfriend named Delilah. The Philistines promised her a lot of money if she would find out what made Samson so strong and help them capture him. She begged Samson to tell her the secret of his strength. He told her he would be weak if he was tied up with leather bowstrings. She tied him up, and then said, "The Philistines are coming!" But he snapped the leather thongs easily.

Delilah tried again. Samson said he could be tied with new ropes. But again he broke the ropes with no trouble. Next he said, "If you weave my hair into a loom, I can't get away." But again he got loose very easily.

Delilah nagged Samson until he told her his

secret. "If my hair is cut, I will be no stronger than other men." Delilah knew he was telling the truth, so she sent for the Philistines. They brought the money and hid nearby. While Samson was asleep, a man came and cut off his hair. Then Delilah called, "Samson! The Philistines are coming!" This time Samson couldn't escape.

DAY 124

Samson's Enemies Capture Him

Judges 16

The Philistines took Samson to a prison in Gaza. They blinded him and chained him up. Samson had to grind the grain for the prison. But Samson's hair began to grow again!

The Philistines decided to have a big celebration and make sacrifices to their god, Dagon, because they thought Dagon had helped them capture Samson. The people got drunk and had Samson brought before them, led by a young boy. Samson stood in the centre of the temple, which was crowded with thousands of jeering Philistines. "Put one of my hands on each large pillar," he told the boy. Then Samson prayed, "O God, please give me back my strength just one more time, so I can punish the Philistines for taking away my sight."

Samson started to push very hard on the two pillars. He cried out, "Let me die with the Philistines!" And the temple collapsed, crushing all the people, including Samson himself. In his death Samson killed more Philistines than he had during his whole life.

146

Naomi and Ruth

Ruth 1

There was a famine in Judah, so a man called Elimelech took his wife, Naomi, and his two sons to Moab to find food. After a while Elimelech died. When his sons grew up, they married Moabite girls named Orpah and Ruth. But both the sons died too, leaving Naomi without any men to care for her.

When she heard that the famine was over, she decided to return to Judah. She tried to send her daughters-in-law back to their parents. Orpah agreed to go, but Ruth insisted on going with her mother-in-law. Ruth said, "I want to stay with you and your people. And I want to worship your God."

So Naomi agreed, and they walked to her hometown, Bethlehem. The village women saw her and asked, "Isn't that Naomi?"

"Don't call me that," Naomi said. "That name means 'pleasant'. My name should be 'Mara', which means 'bitter', because my life has been really bitter. I went to Moab with a husband and sons, but I have come back without them. God has turned his back on me."

155

Hannah Prays for a Son

1 Samuel 1

Elkanah lived with his two wives, Hannah and Peninnah. He loved Hannah best, but she had no children, which made her very sad. Peninnah had several children. She made fun of Hannah and treated her unkindly.

Each year Elkanah took his family to the tabernacle at Shiloh to make his sacrifices and worship God. Year after year Peninnah would say cruel things to Hannah. Hannah was so unhappy that she couldn't eat or sleep, and she would cry bitterly because she was childless.

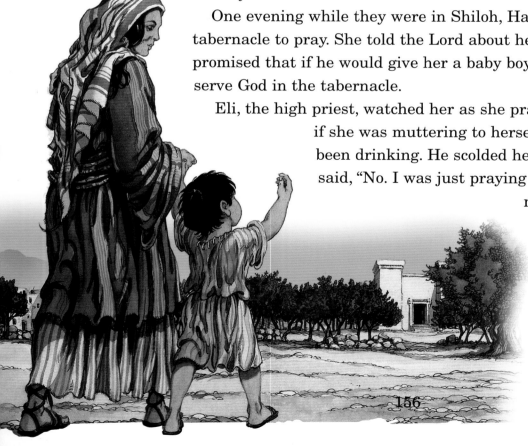

One evening while they were in Shiloh, Hannah went to the tabernacle to pray. She told the Lord about her sadness, and she promised that if he would give her a baby boy, she would let her son serve God in the tabernacle.

Eli, the high priest, watched her as she prayed. Because it looked as if she was muttering to herself, he thought she had been drinking. He scolded her for being drunk, but she said, "No. I was just praying for something I want very much."

Then Eli said, "May God give you exactly what you prayed for!" Hannah went home feeling much better.

156

Israel Asks for a King

1 Samuel 7–8

The people of Israel wondered why they couldn't defeat the Philistines once and for all. Samuel told them it was because they had idols in their homes. He begged them to be sorry for their sin and to get rid of the idols, so they did. Then God gave them victory over the Philistines. Samuel led the people faithfully all of his life. When Samuel became old, he appointed his sons to be judges in his place. But Samuel's sons were dishonest and unfair. So the leaders of Israel said to Samuel, "You are too old to be our judge, and your sons are bad men. Find us a king to rule us."

Samuel didn't like the idea. He asked God what to do. God said, "Give them what they want. But warn them about what will happen if they have a king."

So Samuel warned the people, "You'll be sorry! A king will rule over you and take your money and the best of your crops and herds – even your sons and daughters. You will be like slaves."

But the people refused to listen. "We don't care. We want a king to help us defeat our enemies!"

God Chooses Saul to Be King

1 Samuel 9–10

God promised to help Samuel find the right king. He said, "I'll send you a man from the tribe of Benjamin." Meanwhile, a handsome, young man named Saul was hunting for some lost donkeys. After a long time Saul said to his servant, "We'd better give up and go home. My father will be worried about us."

His servant replied, "Let's just ask the man of God who lives here if he can help us."

So they went to the town where Samuel lived. Samuel saw them coming, and God told him, "That's the man to be king."

Samuel introduced himself to Saul and said, "Your father's donkeys have been found. Now, you are going to be very great in Israel!"

Saul said, "I'm from the smallest tribe, and my family isn't important. How can I be 'great'?"

Samuel explained to Saul that God had chosen him to be king. He poured oil over Saul's head, which showed that God had appointed him for a special service. Later Samuel announced to the country that Saul was to be their king, and all the people shouted, "Long live the king!"

DAY 139

Samuel Warns the People

1 Samuel 11–12

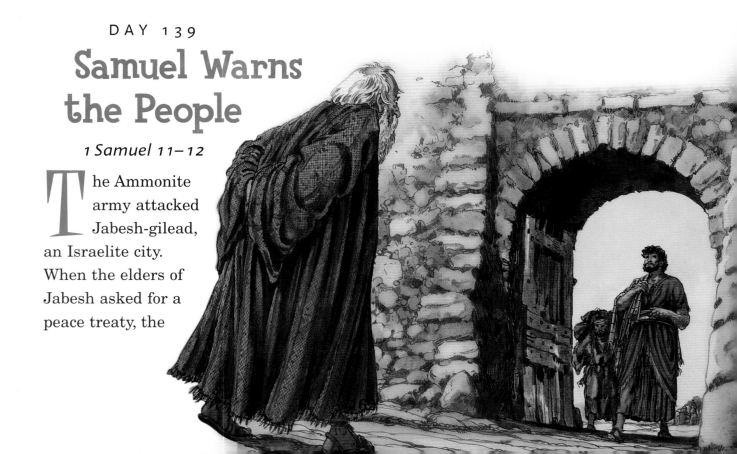

The Ammonite army attacked Jabesh-gilead, an Israelite city. When the elders of Jabesh asked for a peace treaty, the

David to Be the Next King

1 Samuel 15–16

Saul felt terrible when he heard that because of his sin God was going to give Israel a new king. He grabbed Samuel's robe, and it tore. Samuel said, "That's the way the kingdom is going to be torn out of your hands!"

Saul and Samuel worshipped together one more time, then went to their homes, never to see one another again.

God told Samuel to go to Bethlehem and see Jesse. "One of his sons is to be the next king. Invite Jesse to worship with you."

Samuel looked carefully at Jesse's sons when they came with their father to worship. They were all fine, strong men, but God told Samuel, "None of these is

68

the one I've chosen. I don't choose people because of the way they look. I decide because of what's in their hearts."

Samuel asked Jesse if he had any other sons. Jesse said, "Only David, my youngest."

"Call him," Samuel ordered. David came in, a handsome young fellow.

"That's the one!" God said to Samuel. Samuel poured oil on David's head, showing everyone that he was to be the next king. And God sent his Spirit into David's heart.

DAY 143

David Plays for King Saul

1 Samuel 16

Saul proved to be a disobedient king, so God took his Spirit away from Saul and allowed a bad, tormenting spirit to come into his heart, which made Saul nervous, sad, and fearful.

Saul's advisors suggested that music might make him feel better. And Saul liked that idea.

One of the servants said, "David, one of Jesse's sons, plays the harp beautifully. He learned to play out in the fields while he was watching his father's flock of sheep. He's a good musician, and the Lord is with him."

Saul asked Jesse to send David. Jesse sent David to Saul, along with a lot of gifts. Saul liked David from the start and appointed him to be his personal musician. Each time Saul felt the evil spirit coming into his heart, he asked David to play the harp. The music would calm Saul down and the troublesome spirit would leave him for a while. When Saul didn't need him, David would spend time helping Jesse with the sheep, and Saul would almost forget about him.

Goliath Frightens the Israelites

1 Samuel 17

The Philistines decided to attack again, so the two armies got ready for war. The Philistines were in the hills on one side of a valley, and the Israelite army was on the other side of the valley.

The Philistines had a giant in their army – he was more than nine feet tall. The giant named Goliath was amazingly strong. He wore metal armour that weighed over one hundred pounds! He carried a big, thick spear with a fifteen pound tip. Another soldier walked in front of him, carrying a big shield to protect him.

Goliath wasn't afraid of anybody. He laughed at the Israelite soldiers. He shouted, "You don't all need to get killed. Send out just one soldier to fight with me. If he can kill me, the Philistines will be your servants. But if I kill him, then you will have to serve us! Come on, isn't anyone brave enough to fight me?"

Saul was afraid of Goliath, and so were all of his soldiers. No one had the courage to walk out into the valley and tangle with a giant! So they stayed in their camp while Goliath kept daring them to fight.

are depending on your weapons, but I'm depending on the Lord. I will kill you and cut off your head, and everyone will know it was because of my God's power."

Then David ran toward Goliath, swinging his sling. David let a stone fly. It hit the giant in the forehead, and David used Goliath's sword to cut off his head.

When the Philistines saw their greatest warrior fall dead, they ran away. The Israelite soldiers chased them back into their own territory, killing many of them.

Saul made David an officer in his army.

DAY 147

Saul is Jealous

1 Samuel 18

David became a great hero after he killed Goliath and a very successful soldier in Saul's army. Saul was jealous because David was so popular. Saul worried that David would take the kingdom away from him.

The next day the evil spirit came back and bothered Saul again. David began to play the harp to try to quiet Saul, but Saul threw a spear at David. David dodged it. This happened again, but again David jumped aside, and the spear missed him.

Saul thought he would send David to fight the Philistines, then maybe David

would be killed. Saul said, "I promised you my oldest daughter for killing Goliath, but first you must go out and win a battle." While David was out fighting, Saul gave that daughter in marriage to another man.

David came back unharmed. He and another of Saul's daughters, Michal, wanted to get married, but Saul said, "No, first you must kill one hundred Philistines." David went out and killed two hundred of them, so Saul had to let Michal marry him. And the people loved David more and more.

David's Best Friend

1 Samuel 18; 20

David and Saul's son, Jonathan, became the best of friends. David asked Jonathan why the king wanted to kill him. Jonathan replied, "I don't think he would kill you – but I'll find out and let you know."

David said, "King Saul would like to see me dead. Tomorrow is the feast of the new moon. I'll stay away from the court, and you can find out what your father thinks of me."

"All right," Jonathan answered. "If he's as angry as you think, I'll come out here and shoot some arrows into the field. I'll call to my helper, 'The arrows are farther out in the field.' Then you will know you are in danger."

As they parted, David and Jonathan made a promise that they would always take care of each other's families.

At the feast, Jonathan found out that his father was really jealous enough to kill David, so Jonathan went out to the field and gave the signal he and David had agreed upon. David sadly said goodbye and left to escape from Saul.

David Tells a Lie

1 Samuel 21

David left Saul's court so quickly that he didn't take his weapons or any food with him. He went to Nob, where the ark of the covenant was being kept, and visited Ahimelech, the priest. David lied to Ahimelech. He said, "Saul has sent me on a

So Jonathan went out to the field and gave the signal

176

secret mission. I need some supplies for my men who are waiting nearby. Do you have any bread?"

Ahimelech answered, "I don't have any regular bread, but I can give you some of the special bread from the altar if you and your men have been obeying the Law."

"Yes, we have," said David. "And do you have a sword I may use? My business for the king made me leave so quickly that I couldn't bring my own."

"The only sword here is the one that belonged to Goliath. You could take that."

Doeg, Saul's head herdsman, overheard David's conversation with Ahimelech. He hurried back to Saul's court and told him he had seen David at Nob, talking to the priest.

DAY 150

The Result of the Lie

1 Samuel 22

When Doeg told Saul what he had seen at Nob, Saul was furious and blamed Ahimelech for helping David. He sent for Ahimelech and the other priests. He yelled at Ahimelech for helping David escape and giving him supplies. Ahimelech said, "I didn't know he was lying to me. I thought I was doing the right thing to help the king's son-in-law."

The king roared at him, "Don't make excuses! You will die – you and all your family and the other priests too." Saul ordered his soldiers to kill the priests, but they were afraid to harm God's appointed priests, so they refused.

Then Saul ordered Doeg to do it, and Doeg obeyed. He killed eighty-five priests, then went to Nob and killed Ahimelech's relatives and his livestock. Only one son,

Abiathar, escaped. He found David and told him what had happened to Ahimelech and the other priests.

David was heartbroken to think that his selfish lie had caused such terrible trouble. He was sorry he had not trusted God to take care of him instead of lying to protect himself.

DAY 151

David Spares Saul's Life

1 Samuel 23–24

David had about four hundred followers. When he heard that the Philistines were causing trouble again, he asked God if he should fight them. God said yes, so they had a battle at Keilah. David's men won.

When Saul heard about it, he said, "Now I can catch David while he's in Keilah." David heard that Saul was coming after him, and David asked the Lord whether he was in danger. The Lord said he was, so David and his army left the city and travelled around, hiding wherever they could.

From then on, Saul kept trying to find David so he could kill him. But God always warned David in time. More than once David had a chance to kill Saul, but David wouldn't do it, even when his own men said he should.

"No," David said, "it would be wrong for me to harm the man God has chosen as king."

Once David and his men found Saul and his soldiers sleeping in a cave. David crept up quietly and cut off a bit of Saul's robe without waking him. But he would never hurt the king.

Nabal Insults David

1 Samuel 25

For a while David and his men lived in a desert area where there was a rich sheep owner named Nabal. David's soldiers were friendly with Nabal's shepherds and were careful never to steal any of Nabal's sheep. Once David sent this message to Nabal: "We are in need of some supplies, for it is a feast time for us. Would you be so kind as to give us whatever food you can spare?"

Nabal was a mean, unpleasant man, and he answered crossly, "Why should I give my valuable food to someone who may be a runaway or a criminal for all I know? Forget it!"

This answer made David angry, so he went to teach Nabal a lesson. Meanwhile, one of Nabal's shepherds hurried to Nabal's wife, Abigail, who was gentle and kind and very beautiful. He told her how kind David's men had been to them and how rude Nabal had been to David's messenger.

Abigail realised they were in danger because of Nabal's insults, so she thought of a plan. Could she save them from David's anger?

David Marries Abigail

1 Samuel 25

Abigail prepared some food for David and his men – bread, wine, sheep ready for cooking, roasted grain, and cakes of raisins and dried figs. She loaded it all onto donkeys and sent servants on ahead. Abigail followed.

Abigail met David as he approached Nabal's farm. She bowed low before him.

She said, "Sir, I apologise for my husband's rudeness. He is a wicked, foolish man. Please forgive us and accept this food. I know God has blessed you and will make you the king of Israel. Surely you would not want to have Nabal's death on your conscience."

David's heart was touched, and he answered, "Of course I accept your apology. Thank you for your gift. Go back home in peace."

Abigail went home, and the next day she told Nabal how she had prevented David from killing him. Nabal was so shocked that he became very ill and couldn't move. Ten days later, he died.

When David heard that Nabal was dead, he sent his men to bring Abigail to his camp, and they were married.

DAY 154

David Refuses to Kill the King

1 Samuel 26

Once when Saul was looking for him, David and his nephew Abishai crept over to Saul's camp at night. Saul was asleep, with Abner, his general, beside him. The other soldiers lay around them, to protect them. Saul's spear was stuck into the ground beside his head. Abishai whispered to David, "God has given us a good chance to get rid of your enemy."

"No!" David answered. "God made him king, and it would be wrong to kill him. Just take his spear and water bottle, and let's get out of here."

No one saw them or heard them. When they were a safe distance away, David shouted, "Hey, Abner! Wake up! You haven't been taking very good care of the king. Where are his spear and his water jar?"

Saul recognised David's voice, and he called, "Is that you, David?"

"Yes, my lord. Tell me what I've done to deserve your anger. I would never hurt you."

Then Saul told David he was sorry. Saul said, "Come on home now, and I won't hurt you." But David didn't trust Saul, so David went away and Saul went home.

Saul Calls Samuel's Spirit

1 Samuel 28

David realised that Saul might chase him forever, so he asked Achish, a Philistine leader, for a city to live in. In return, he would help Achish with his wars. David, his men, and their families settled in the city of Ziklag.

After a while some of the Philistines prepared to attack Saul's army. Saul asked God what to do but got no answer. Saul used to get advice from the Lord through Samuel, but Samuel had died. Saul wanted to try to talk to Samuel's spirit, but he himself had made a law against trying to get messages from the dead. He was so desperate that he disguised himself and went to Endor, where there was a woman who thought she could talk to dead people.

Even she was surprised when Samuel appeared! Then she guessed that her visitor was the king, and she was terrified.

Saul asked Samuel what he should do about the Philistines. Samuel said, "You got yourself into this when you disobeyed God. Now God will give David the kingdom. And when you fight with the Philistines, they will win. Tomorrow you will be dead."

David Defeats the Amalekites

1 Samuel 29–30

David and his men expected to fight with the Philistines against Saul's army. But some of the Philistine leaders didn't trust David. "He'll probably change sides when we start fighting." So David took his men back to Ziklag, only to find that the Amalekite army had burned the city and had taken the women and children – including David's two wives.

David asked God, "If I catch up with the Amalekites, can I defeat them and get our families back?"

God said, "Yes, go! You will get back everything they have stolen."

So David and his men started out. Some of the soldiers stayed behind. The rest of them soon caught up to the Amalekites and fought fiercely with them. At last David and his men killed almost all the enemy and were able to take their wives and children and property home.

When they rejoined the soldiers who had stayed behind, some of David's men said, "They don't deserve any of the loot because they didn't help with the fighting."

David said, "No, that's not fair, and after all, the Lord is the one who gives us the victory!"

Israel's First King Dies

1 Samuel 31

The Philistines overpowered the Israelites and killed many of them, including Saul's sons. Saul was wounded very badly. He said to his armour bearer, "Please kill me so that the Philistines won't capture me and torture me."

But his armour bearer couldn't do it, so Saul took his own life by making himself fall against the point of his sword. The Philistines chased the Israelites out of their towns and occupied them.

When the Philistine soldiers went out onto the battlefield to steal things from the bodies of the dead soldiers, they found the bodies of Saul and his sons. The Philistines cut off their heads and displayed them on the wall of one of their cities to show their disrespect for the Israelite king.

When the Israelites heard that, they came and took away the bodies. The Israelites cremated them and buried the ashes; then they mourned for their king for seven days.

David is Crowned King

2 Samuel 1–4

David was sorry when he heard that Saul and Jonathan were dead. David asked God, "Should I move back to Judah?" and God said yes. So David and his men and their families settled in the city of Hebron. The leaders of Judah crowned David king of their tribe.

Meanwhile, Saul's army commander, Abner, chose Saul's son Ishbosheth to be king of the other tribes of Israel. So God's people were divided into two groups, each with its own king. For years they fought, each trying to take control of the whole nation.

Gradually David's group became the stronger. Abner and Ishbosheth quarrelled, and Abner offered to surrender Israel's forces to David in exchange for being made commander of the combined army.

Joab, one of David's chief soldiers, hated Abner, so without David's knowing it, he murdered Abner. Then Ishbosheth was killed by two of his army captains. They bragged about it to David. David was angry. He had wanted always to be fair to Saul's family, so David had the assassins killed.

DAY 159

God Punishes Uzzah

2 Samuel 5–6

With the army of Israel united and strong, David drove the Jebusites out of Jerusalem. Then he made it his capital city. Next, David defeated the Philistines.

David wanted the ark back where it belonged, so he went to the town where it had been held for many years. The ark was placed on a new oxcart, and two men, Uzzah and Ahio, walked beside it. When one of the oxen stumbled, Uzzah put out his hand and held the ark steady.

God had said that men must never touch the ark. They must move it by lifting it with poles. So when Uzzah touched the ark, God was angry with Uzzah and struck him dead. David said, "I'm afraid to keep on moving the ark. We'll leave it here, at the home of Obed-edom."

The ark was there for three months, and during that time God greatly blessed Obed-edom and his family. When David saw this, he decided it was time to go back and get the ark and take it home.

The Ark Returns to Jerusalem

2 Samuel 6

David went to the home of Obed-edom and got the ark. He and the people with him started the trip to Jerusalem. They were so happy that they sang and danced and shouted for joy as they travelled along.

As they entered Jerusalem, David danced and sang more than anyone else. His wife Michal, Saul's daughter, watched the procession from the window. She thought the way David was acting was disgusting.

At last the ark was back where it belonged, and David made more sacrifices. Then he blessed the people in the name of the Lord and gave everyone a gift of bread, raisins, and dates.

David went home to give blessings to his own family. But Michal didn't feel like celebrating. She said, "You really made a fool of yourself today, jumping around without your royal robe – in public!"

David replied, "Look, I was dancing before the Lord, not to get the attention of people. God chose me to be king. I would be willing to look even more foolish than I did today to express my thanks to God!"

DAY 161

David's Kindness to Jonathan's Family

2 Samuel 9

David missed Jonathan and wanted to do something to honour his memory. He remembered how he and Jonathan had promised to take care of each other's families if either of them should die. David sent for Ziba, an old servant of Saul's, and asked him if any members of Saul's household were still alive.

The servant said, "Yes, one of Jonathan's sons is alive. He is Mephibosheth, who was crippled when he was a little boy."

So David sent for Mephibosheth. "Don't be afraid of me," David said. "I loved your father, Jonathan, and I want to be kind to you for his sake. I'll give back your family's land, but I want you to come and live here at the palace with me."

Then David said to Ziba, "I've given all of Saul's land to Mephibosheth. I want you and your family to farm Mephibosheth's land so his family will have plenty of food. But he is going to live at the palace as my guest for the rest of his life."

David and Bathsheba

2 Samuel 11

David's army was at war with the Ammonites, but David stayed in Jerusalem. One night as he walked around on the palace roof David saw, in a nearby home, a beautiful woman bathing. She was Bathsheba, the wife of Uriah, one of David's army officers.

David sent for her and slept with her as if she were his wife. She became pregnant.

David didn't want anyone to know he was the baby's father. He told Uriah to go home so that it would look as if Uriah had been with his wife and the baby was his. But Uriah refused. He said, "My duty is to stay with the army."

David decided to get rid of Uriah so that he could marry Bathsheba. David told General Joab to send Uriah into a part of the fighting where he would almost certainly be killed. So Joab put Uriah on the front line and then pulled the other soldiers back, leaving Uriah to die. Joab sent the news of his death to David.

David married Bathsheba, and soon she had a baby boy.

The Baby Dies

2 Samuel 12

God was angry with David because he had committed adultery and murder. He sent a prophet named Nathan to David. Nathan told David this story: "Once two men were neighbours. One was very rich and had many sheep and cattle.

The other was poor; he had only one little ewe lamb, which was almost like one of the family. Once the rich man had a guest. Instead of killing one of his own sheep, he stole the poor man's lamb and cooked it for his guest's dinner."

David was terribly angry. He said, "Why, a selfish man like that should be killed."

Nathan said, "David, you are that rich man. God has been good to you. He made you king over Israel and Judah. You have everything you need, yet you have stolen Uriah's wife and then murdered him."

David confessed that he had sinned against God. Nathan said that because he was sorry, he would not have to die, but Bathsheba's baby would die. In a few days the baby became very sick, and although David prayed for him, the baby died.

DAY 164

A Rebellious Son

2 Samuel 13–15

David had married several women, so he had children who were half brothers and half sisters. Some of them were jealous of one another and quarrelled a lot. Once David's oldest son, Amnon, hurt the sister of his half brother Absalom. Absalom was furious. He told his servants to kill Amnon – which was as bad as doing the killing himself. Absalom had to run away to keep David from punishing him, and he stayed away for three years.

David had been angry with Absalom, but he missed his son. Joab persuaded him to allow Absalom to return home.

Absalom lived in Jerusalem for two years, but his father refused to see him. Finally Absalom asked Joab to get David to change his mind. So David let Absalom come and see him.

This did not heal the trouble between them. Absalom didn't forgive his father for not accepting him. He decided to try to get the kingdom away from David. He was a fine-looking young man, with long thick hair that he cut only once a year. People liked him, and he went to Hebron and gathered a lot of followers.

DAY 165

David Runs Away from His Son

2 Samuel 15–17

When David realised how popular Absalom had become, he thought, I'd better get out of Jerusalem before he comes after me to kill me. David's friend Hushai wanted to go with him, but David asked him to stay and send him news of what Absalom was doing. So Hushai stayed, but David and his soldiers hid in the wilderness.

Soon afterward, Absalom and his army entered the city. His advisor said, "Let's chase after David and kill him. Then the people will make you king in his place."

Hushai pretended to be loyal to Absalom, so Absalom asked Hushai what he thought. Hushai said, "You had better wait and gather a much larger army." He said this to give David more time to escape. Then he sent a message to David, telling him what Absalom was planning.

Some of Absalom's spies saw the messengers and chased them. But a man hid

Solomon Makes a Wise Decision

1 Kings 3

In a dream one night, Solomon told God he wanted wisdom more than anything else. God said, "I am going to give you wisdom, and riches and honour too, even though you didn't ask for them."

One day two women came to ask Solomon to settle a quarrel.

One said, "This other woman and I each had a baby. Her baby died, but in the night she took my baby and left her dead baby in my bed. I knew that the dead child was hers, but she wouldn't give back my baby."

The other woman said, "That's not true! The dead baby is hers, and the living baby is mine."

Solomon tested them. He took a sword, held up the living baby, and said, "We'll cut the baby in two and give half to each woman."

One of the women agreed, but the real mother cried out, "No! Give him to her! I'd rather give him up than let him be killed."

Then Solomon said, "Give the baby to the one who wants his life spared. She is the real mother."

Everyone could see how wise God had made Solomon.

DAY 171

Solomon Builds God's Temple

1 Kings 5–7; 9

Solomon was eager to build a temple as a permanent house for God. King Hiram of Tyre offered to help. He sent beautiful cedar and cypress logs, and Solomon paid him by providing food for his workmen. Solomon sent men to help with the logging while others cut big blocks of stone from quarries.

After they had prepared all the materials, the building began. All the stone had been cut to the right size at the quarry. The inside of the walls was lined with the cedar boards; then everything was covered with gold – even the ceiling and the cypress floors were bright gold.

Like the tabernacle, the Temple had a special inner room called the Most Holy Place. Everything in the room was covered with pure gold. There the ark was kept, and the gold-covered altar. Beside the ark were two very large carved figures of cherubs.

The Temple was a beautiful house for God. The Lord said to Solomon, "As long as you obey me and live as you should, I will live here among your people and will never abandon you."

God's Glory Fills the Temple

1 Kings 7–8

Next, all the furnishings for the Temple were made. Skilful craftsmen made basins, pots, shovels, tanks, latticework, and pillars. They did beautiful carving in the wood panelling, then overlaid it with gold. Everything was made as perfectly as possible because it was for the house of God.

After seven years, everything was finished. Solomon called the people together for a big celebration. The priests carried the ark from the tabernacle and placed it in the Most Holy Place, with the wings of the two large cherubs shadowing its cover. As the priests came out of the Most Holy Place, the glory of God came and filled the Temple like a huge cloud.

King Solomon blessed the people and then prayed. He dedicated the Temple to God's service and promised that he and his people would always worship God faithfully.

Then he sacrificed thousands of animals as a peace offering. He and the people celebrated for fourteen days. Their hearts were full of joy and thanksgiving for God's blessings to them.

The Kingdom is Divided

1 Kings 11–12

Ahijah, a prophet, met Jeroboam, one of Solomon's officials. Ahijah took off his coat and tore it into twelve pieces. Ahijah handed ten pieces to Jeroboam and said, "The Lord is going to make you the king of ten tribes of Israel. Only the tribes of Judah and Benjamin will stay in Solomon's family after his death."

Solomon heard about this and tried to kill Jeroboam. But Jeroboam escaped.

After Solomon had been king for forty years, he died. His son Rehoboam became king.

Jeroboam returned for the ceremony.

He made trouble for Rehoboam by getting some people to ask the new king, "Are you going to be as hard on us as Solomon was, or will you be more kind?"

Rehoboam wasn't sure how to answer, so he asked for advice. Older people told him to answer pleasantly, but young men advised him to get tough. Rehoboam took the young men's advice, and this made the people angry.

They said, "We don't want this mean fellow to be our king. Let Rehoboam rule his own little family tribe. We'll get Jeroboam to rule the rest of the country." This was just what God had planned.

Jeroboam Builds Idols

1 Kings 12–13

God's people were divided into two different nations: Israel was ruled by Jeroboam and Judah by Rehoboam. Rehoboam thought he should fight to reunite the kingdom, but God said no.

Jeroboam set up his capital at Shechem. He thought, "If my people go to the Temple in Jerusalem, they may want to be part of Judah and give their loyalty to Rehoboam. I'd better make them a place to worship here in Israel."

Then he committed a great sin. He formed two golden calves and set up one in Dan and the other in Bethel.

He made shrines all over the countryside and appointed new priests who were not Levites. He also set new times for feasts and festivals, ignoring the rules God had given the people for proper worship.

God sent a prophet from Judah to Jeroboam, who was making an offering.

The prophet said, "One of the kings of Judah will kill these false priests. To prove it, God will split this altar in two."

Jeroboam was angry. He pointed to the prophet and yelled, "Grab him!" Instantly the king's hand was paralysed, and the altar split in two.

A Lion Kills a Prophet

1 Kings 13

Jeroboam begged the prophet to pray for him. The prophet asked God to heal Jeroboam, and immediately his hand was all right. Jeroboam invited the prophet to eat at his home. The prophet said, "No, God told me I must not eat or drink anything here." He started back to Judah.

Another old prophet lived in Bethel. He heard about the prophet from Judah and what had happened to Jeroboam. He rode after the prophet from Judah and invited him home for a meal. The prophet from Judah refused, "God has forbidden me to eat or drink anything in Israel."

Then the old prophet lied. He said, "I am a prophet, and God told me it would be all right." The prophet from Judah believed him and went to the old prophet's home and had a meal. Then the Lord gave the old prophet this message for the prophet from Judah: "You have disobeyed me. Therefore your body will not be buried with your ancestors." The prophet from Judah started for home again. But a lion killed him along the road. His body was taken back to Bethel and buried, far away from his family burial place.

Jeroboam's Son Dies

1 Kings 14

Jeroboam had a little boy named Abijah, who became very sick. Jeroboam told his wife, "Go in disguise to the prophet, Ahijah, who told me I would be king. Ask him what will happen to our son."

Drought and Famine

1 Kings 18

After three more years of drought, God told Elijah to go to King Ahab and tell him God was going to end the drought. Meanwhile, the king and Obadiah, one of his officers, went out to look for some grass for their horses and mules. The king said, "Let's separate. We must find food to save these animals from starvation."

Obadiah met Elijah and recognised him. Elijah said, "I'm on my way to the palace to see Ahab. Please tell him I am coming."

"I can't," Obadiah groaned. "The king has been looking for you everywhere. If I tell him you are coming and God sends you somewhere else, he will be furious. He'll probably kill me!"

Elijah said, "Don't worry. I won't disappear again." When Ahab heard that Elijah was coming, he went out to meet him. He yelled, "So, there you are, you troublemaker."

Elijah answered, "No! You are the troublemaker because you turned your back on God and worshipped Baal and other false gods."

A Contest on Mount Carmel

1 Kings 18

Elijah decided to prove to the people of Israel who their true God really was. He said to King Ahab, "Call all the people to Mount Carmel. Bring the 450 prophets of Baal with you and the 400 prophets of Asherah."

Then Elijah spoke to the people of Israel: "How long are you going to say you are God's people but worship Baal? If God is the true God, then worship him. But if Baal is really God, then follow him."

Then Elijah said, "I'm the only one of God's prophets left alive. Baal has 450 prophets. Let them take a bull for sacrifice and cut it up and put it on their altar, but don't light the fire. Then let them pray to Baal, and if he is really God, he will send fire to burn up the sacrifice."

The people all said, "That's a good idea."

So the 450 prophets began to pray to Baal, but nothing happened. They danced around; they even cut themselves with knives, but Baal didn't answer them, because he was just an idol. Elijah made fun of them, "Maybe your god is asleep or taking a trip!" But still nothing happened.

DAY 184

Fire from Heaven

1 Kings 18

Then it was Elijah's turn. He gathered the people around him. He chose twelve large stones to represent the twelve tribes of Israel, and he repaired the broken-down altar of the Lord. Then he dug a ditch around it.

He killed a bull, cut it into pieces, and put the pieces on the altar. Three times he poured water over the altar so that it covered the sacrifice and filled the ditch around the altar.

Everything was ready. Elijah stood before the altar and prayed, "O Lord, you are a faithful God. Prove to these people that you are indeed the one true God so they will worship you again."

Instantly, fire swooped down from heaven and burned up the sacrifice, the wood,

217

and the stones. It even dried up all the water in the ditch. The people all fell down on their faces and cried out, "Almighty God is the true God!"

Elijah told the people to grab the prophets of Baal. They took them to the Kishon Valley, and there Elijah killed all the false prophets.

God Sends Rain at Last

1 Kings 18

After Elijah had informed King Ahab that rain was on the way, he climbed to the top of Mount Carmel and knelt down. He said to his servant, "Look out toward the sea; then tell me what you see."

The servant came back and said, "I don't see anything."

Elijah said, "Go again." He said this to his servant seven times.

Finally the servant returned and reported, "I see a very small cloud on the horizon. It's no larger than a man's hand."

"Good!" said Elijah. "Now go and tell Ahab that he'd better

drive quickly down the mountain. Soon the rain will be so heavy he won't be able to make the trip."

Even as he spoke, the small cloud grew larger. In just moments the sky became black with storm clouds. The wind blew fiercely, and then the rain came. It poured! King Ahab was riding in his chariot to the city. God gave Elijah the strength to run faster than Ahab's chariot, and Elijah reached the city first!

DAY 186

An Angel Feeds Elijah

1 Kings 19

As soon as Ahab got home, he told Queen Jezebel everything that had happened on Mount Carmel. When he got to the part about how Elijah had killed all the prophets of Baal, she became terribly angry. She sent this message to Elijah: "By this time tomorrow, I will see to it that you are dead."

Elijah was afraid she would kill him, so he fled from the city. He travelled out into the desert,

Elijah was surprised to see some fresh bread and a jar of water on a rock nearby.

219

where, he hoped, Jezebel couldn't find him.

That night he told God, "You might as well take my life." Then he fell asleep.

An angel came and woke him. "Get up and eat," the angel said. Elijah was surprised to see some fresh bread and a jar of water on a rock nearby. He ate and drank, then went back to sleep. Again the angel came. "Come and eat some more. You need strength for a long journey."

Again Elijah ate, and then he set out. He went to Mount Sinai, where he camped in a cave.

God Chooses a New Prophet

1 Kings 19

God asked Elijah what he was doing on Mount Sinai. Elijah said, "I've been trying to serve you well. I'm the only true believer left, and now your people want to kill me, too." God answered, "Step outside the cave, Elijah, and stand before me as I pass by." Elijah stood on the mountain, and a strong wind blew by, but that wasn't the Lord.

Then an earthquake shook the land, but God wasn't in the earthquake. A fire came, but still God didn't pass by.

Finally Elijah heard a small, quiet voice, and he knew God had come.

The voice said, "Elijah, why are you here?"

Again Elijah told God he was the only faithful believer left in Israel. God replied, "Listen Elijah. You are not alone! There are seven thousand people who have never worshipped Baal. Now I want you to anoint a new king for Syria and one for Israel. Then find a man named Elisha. He will help you, and later he will take your place."

Elijah found Elisha ploughing in a field. Elijah threw his cloak around Elisha's shoulders. Elisha knew this meant he was to be Elijah's successor. He went home and celebrated with his family; then he joined Elijah and worked with him.

A Victory for Israel

1 Kings 20

King Ben-hadad of Aram planned to attack Samaria, the Israelite capital. He sent this message to King Ahab: "Give me your wives and children, silver and gold!" Ahab was afraid, so he agreed.

Then Ben-hadad sent another message: "My men will take whatever they want from your palace and your people's homes."

Ahab's advisors said, "Stand up to him!" So Ahab refused Ben-hadad's demand.

That made Ben-hadad angry. He sent this message to Ahab: "By tomorrow, Samaria will be just a pile of trash."

Ahab was feeling braver, so he replied, "Don't brag about it until you've done it!"

The Aramean army prepared to attack. Meanwhile, a prophet told Ahab, "The Lord will help you win. Then you will know he is the true God. Take part of your army and go out to meet the Arameans."

The battle started. The Israelites killed a great many Arameans. The rest panicked and ran away.

The next spring the Arameans attacked again, but again they were defeated. Ahab agreed not to kill Ben-hadad.

The prophet told Ahab that God would punish him because he had not killed Ben-hadad the way God had told him to.

Naaman is Healed

2 Kings 5

Naaman's servants said, "Oh, sir, don't give up. If the prophet had told you to do something hard, you would have done it. Well, he's told you to do something very easy, so why not try this simple cure?"

So Naaman washed himself in the Jordan River seven times. When he came out the seventh time, the disease was gone!

Naaman was excited and happy. He and his men went back to Elisha's house, and

237

Naaman apologised. He said, "Now I realise that the God of Israel is the one true God. Please take these gifts of gold and silver and the clothing I have brought."

Elisha said, "No. I would never accept payment for what I did. God would not want me to do that." Naaman kept urging him, but Elisha still refused the gifts.

Naaman said, "All right. But I want to take some of the dirt from the ground because when I get home I will always make sacrifices on an altar to the true God. I'll never worship false gods again."

He said goodbye and started back to Aram, thankful to be healed.

DAY 201

A Greedy Servant

2 Kings 5

Gehazi had heard his master refuse Naaman's gifts. After Naaman left, Gehazi thought, What a waste! I think I'll go and get some for myself! Gehazi caught up with Naaman. Naaman asked, "Is something the matter?"

Gehazi answered, "No, but Elisha has two visitors, and he would like to have a bar of silver and two of the sets of clothing to give them."

Naaman believed Gehazi's lie and said, "Of course. I will give you twice as much as you asked for." And he told his servants to put the silver and clothes in bags and carry them home for Gehazi.

When they got there, Gehazi took the bags from the servants and hid them in his own house. Then he went back to Elisha, who asked, "Where have you been, Gehazi?"

"I didn't go anywhere," Gehazi said.

"Listen, because of your greed and your lies and trickery, you and all your descendants are going to have leprosy instead of Naaman."

Immediately Gehazi's skin became white with the terrible disease of leprosy.

The Axe That Floated and the Blind Army

2 Kings 6

The school of the prophets was growing, and their building wasn't large enough. They said to Elisha, "Let's build a new school building."

Elisha agreed, so they went to the riverbank to cut logs. One of the students had borrowed an axe. He was very upset when the iron head of his axe became loose, fell into the river, and sank.

Elisha threw a stick into the water. The axe head floated to the surface, and the young man got it back.

When Aram was at war with Israel, the king of Aram gave some battle plans to one of his generals. Elisha warned the king of Israel about the plans. The Aramean king thought there must be a spy in his troops.

But one of his soldiers said, "No, it's that prophet Elisha. God reveals secrets to him."

"Then we'll kill him," the king said. He sent soldiers to capture Elisha, but God protected Elisha by blinding all the soldiers. Elisha led them into Israel's capital city and then let them see again!

The Israelite king wanted to kill them, but Elisha said no. Instead they fed the soldiers and let them go home.

A Terrible Food Shortage

2 Kings 6–7

King Ben-hadad attacked Samaria. His army surrounded the city and kept any food from being brought in. The people in Samaria became extremely hungry. Some even killed and ate other people.

King Joram decided it was all Elisha's fault. He said, "When I find him, I'm going to kill him." Joram wouldn't admit that the real cause of the fighting and the hunger was his own wickedness. He had forgotten Israel's true God and worshipped idols.

But he was sad to see his people suffering. He wore a rough garment next to his skin to remind himself of their needs.

Elisha heard about the king's threats, so he stayed inside his house. He said to his friends, "Guard the door. Keep the king's messenger outside. Soon the king will come after me himself."

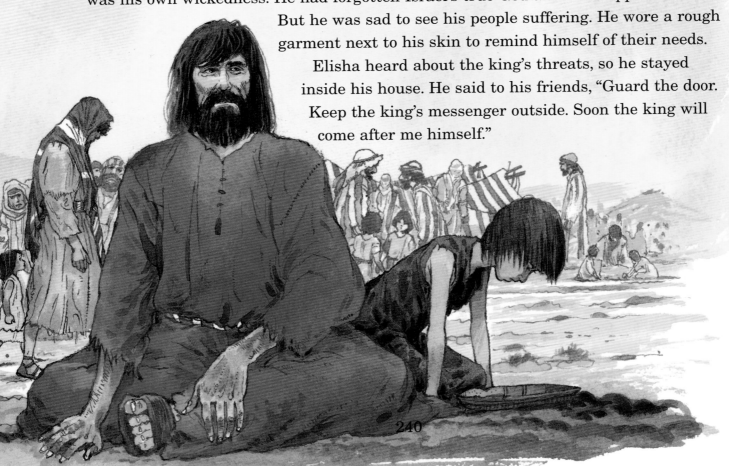

240

When Joram came, Elisha told him that God had promised to end the food shortage the next day. "Food will be so plentiful," he said, "that you'll be able to buy flour and grain for a very low price."

Four Lepers Share with Others

2 Kings 7

Four lepers lived just outside the gate of Samaria. They were starving and said, "Let's go over to the Aramean camp and surrender. If they don't kill us, they might give us a little food."

When the lepers arrived, not a single soldier was there. God had made the Arameans think they were under attack. So they had run away, leaving everything in their camp!

The lepers found a lot of food in one tent, and they ate all they wanted. Then they found clothing and gold and silver. They grabbed everything they could carry and hid it. Then they started back for more.

Suddenly they said, "We

shouldn't be taking all this stuff for ourselves. We should share it with the suffering people in the city."

The lepers hurried back to the gate of Samaria and called to the guards. "We've found a lot of food in the Aramean camp. The soldiers have left; we can take all we want."

When they were sure it wasn't a trap, the people of the city rushed over to the camp and helped themselves.

DAY 205

A Woman Gets Her Land Back

2 Kings 8

The woman whose little boy Elisha brought back to life, took Elisha's advice and left Israel until the famine was over. One day, after the famine had ended, Gehazi, Elisha's servant, was talking to the king.

The king said, "I want to know more about Elisha. Tell me some of the wonderful miracles he has done."

The servant told him about the woman with the little boy. Just then, she and her son walked into the palace. She had come to see the king about getting her land and home back.

Gehazi said, "This is the woman I was telling you about, Your Majesty. And this is the boy who was dead."

The king asked her, "Did all those things really happen to you?"

"Yes," she said. "That's exactly what happened."

So the king arranged for her to get back her house and land. He even gave her money to pay for the crops that had been harvested from her land during the seven years she had been gone.

Jehoash did, and Elisha put his hands over the king's hands. Together they pulled back the bowstring and shot the arrow through an open window.

Elisha said, "This is a sign that Israel is going to be free of the Arameans."

Then the prophet told the king to hit the floor with a bundle of arrows. The king struck the floor three times, then stopped.

Elisha said, "You stopped too soon. Now you will only defeat Aram three times. If you had kept going, you would have kept on defeating the Arameans until they were destroyed."

Elisha died and was buried. One day some men were taking a body to be buried. They saw some robbers coming, so they put the dead man in Elisha's tomb and ran away. As soon as the dead body touched Elisha's bones, the man came back to life again.

Even in death, Elisha could do miracles!

God's Prophets Warn Israel

2 Kings 14; Amos; Hosea

Israel fought and defeated Aram three times. After Jehoash died, his son, Jeroboam II, became king. He, too, was an idol-worshipping king. God now chose new prophets. One of these was Amos, a shepherd. God gave Amos harsh words of warning for the people of Israel.

God said, "The cities of Israel have sinned again and again, and I will not forget it. Now, prepare yourselves for the punishment I will send."

To be sure they understood, God said, "A carpenter uses a plumb line to

248

check how straight a wall is. I have checked you against my plumb line, and you are crooked with sin!"

Then he said they were like ripe fruit, ready to be picked. That meant they were ready to receive his punishment. Hosea scolded the people, too, saying, "You are like a wife who isn't loving and faithful to her husband. You have left God and loved idols instead." Hosea said they were like people who chased the wind. In worshipping idols they were running after something they couldn't even touch because the false gods weren't real.

The Death of a Nation

2 Kings 15–17

Jeroboam II was followed by several other kings, all of them idol worshippers. Not one of the kings of Israel was faithful to God. They all led the people away from true worship.

God had promised Israel that he would bless them and protect them if they were faithful to him. But for more than two hundred years they had been unfaithful, so God took away his protection.

The king of Assyria attacked Israel and forced King Hoshea to pay taxes to Assyria. After a while Hoshea secretly asked the king of Egypt to help free him from Assyria's rule, and he stopped paying the tax money.

The Assyrian king, Shalmaneser, heard about Hoshea's deal with Egypt, and it made him angry.

Shalmaneser grabbed Hoshea and put him in prison. For three years his large army attacked Samaria, the capital of Israel.

Finally the city surrendered. The citizens of Israel became prisoners of war and were shipped off to live in Assyria.

Then Shalmaneser filled up Samaria with people from foreign cities. They were all idol worshippers and cared nothing about God. What a sad thing to happen in the land God had prepared for his own people!

DAY 212

Meanwhile, Back in Judah...

1 Kings 14–15; 2 Chronicles 15–16

After King Solomon died, his kingdom was divided into two groups of tribes. Israel was the larger group, and Judah the smaller. It was bad enough being divided into two kingdoms, but it was even worse when the two kingdoms fought against each other.

During one of those fights, the king of Judah scolded Israel for not having a king from King David's family. He said, "You have a much bigger army than we do, but because you worship the gold calf idols your king made for you, the Lord our God will help us defeat you." And that's just what happened.

One of the kings of Judah was Asa. As long as he trusted God, he could defeat his enemies. But when Asa hired the Aramean army to defend him instead of asking for God's help, God wasn't pleased and sent a prophet to scold him.

The prophet said, "You should have trusted the Lord. From now on, he will let your enemies defeat you."

Asa was disgusted with the prophet and threw him in jail. Then the king became ill and died. Jehoshaphat became the next king of Judah.

had a wise counsellor named Zechariah. God helped Uzziah build Judah into a powerful nation with a strong army.

Later Uzziah's success and power began to change him. One day he entered the Most Holy Place in the Temple, where only priests were allowed to go, and burned incense at the altar. The high priest and other priests told him to get out or the Lord would punish him. Uzziah refused to leave. Soon the skin on his forehead became white and lumpy with leprosy. He remained a leper for the rest of his life, and his son Jotham became king.

DAY 222

Isaiah Says a Saviour Will Come

2 Chronicles 27; Isaiah

Jotham was twenty-five when he was crowned king. He obeyed God and tried to lead the people in the right way. Like his father, he successfully fought against the Ammonites and forced them to pay a lot of money each year, plus 50,000 sacks of wheat and 50,000 sacks of barley.

Even though Jotham obeyed the Lord, most of his people were being disobedient. God sent one of his greatest prophets, Isaiah, to advise them and warn them about their sins.

Through Isaiah, God told them that if they obeyed him he would bless them, but if they worshipped idols, he would leave them and they would have much trouble and sorrow. He warned them that if they carried on disobeying him, enemy tribes would capture them and seize their Promised Land.

Some of Isaiah's prophecy was about Jesus, God's Son, who would become the Saviour of the world. Seven hundred years later these words came true. Isaiah knew what would happen in the future because he was God's prophet and God revealed the future to him.

DAY 223

King Ahaz Nails the Temple Shut

2 Chronicles 28

Jotham died after ruling Judah for sixteen years. He had been faithful to God, but his son Ahaz wasn't like him. When Ahaz became king, he worshipped the false god Baal. But even worse than that, he offered his own children on a heathen altar.

To punish him, God let the Aramean and Israelite armies defeat him in war. Many of his people were taken captive to Aram, and the army of Israel killed thousands of Judah's soldiers, including the king's son.

The Israelites also took away 200,000 women and children from Judah. A prophet rebuked them, saying, "God wants to use you to punish Judah, but you are going too far." Then they let some of the captives go.

Ahaz needed help against his enemies, so he hired troops from King Tiglath-pileser of Assyria. The king helped him defeat Aram and capture Damascus, but then he turned against Ahaz.

Ahaz destroyed some of the beautiful things in the Temple. Finally he nailed the Temple doors shut.

Everywhere the people looked, they saw idols that their king had put up. And God was disappointed in Judah and angry with King Ahaz.

Hezekiah Opens God's House

2 Chronicles 29

Though Ahaz had been a bad king, his son Hezekiah loved God. Hezekiah was king of Judah for twenty-nine years, and he brought the country back to the Lord. In the very first month he was king, Hezekiah opened up the Temple. He called in the Levites and priests and said to them, "Purify yourselves according to the Law, and then clean up God's house of worship."

It took them sixteen days to prepare the Temple for worship. Then they reported to Hezekiah, "Everything is clean and ready for use."

The next day Hezekiah went to the Temple with the leaders of the city. He took many animals for sacrifice. The priests made burnt offerings and sin offerings for all of the people. The king appointed some Levites to be in an orchestra and others to play trumpets, just as it had been done in King David's time. Then they all joined in the worship of God. How happy King Hezekiah and all his people were to be obeying God once again in his holy Temple!

Passover: A Happy Time Again

2 Chronicles 30

For many years the people in Judah had not celebrated the Passover feast that reminded them of the time when God led them out of Egypt. Now Hezekiah was trying to obey all of God's commands, and he wanted the people to celebrate the Passover again. He invited everyone to come to Jerusalem and join in the celebration.

He wanted all the priests and Levites to get ready for it too. Usually the Passover was in April, but because there wasn't enough time to get ready that early, the king decided to have it in May.

What a great time they had! The festival lasted for seven days and was filled with praise and music and reading of God's Word. The people were so happy that they stayed for another week.

When they went back to their homes in different parts of the country, they tore down idols and heathen altars. They wanted their country to be a place where only the true God was worshipped.

DAY 226

An Angel Fights for Judah

2 Chronicles 32

The king of Assyria was planning to attack Jerusalem. Hezekiah encouraged his soldiers. "Don't be afraid! God will protect us." But Hezekiah was afraid of the Assyrians' army. He sent their king some gifts, hoping to get them to call off their attack.

They went away for a while, but later their king sent some soldiers to boast about what he was going to do. They called to the watchmen on the wall, "Don't believe what Hezekiah says about God's protection. You might as well surrender and be our slaves."

Hezekiah prayed and asked the prophet Isaiah to pray too. Isaiah sent the king this message: "Do not be afraid. God will punish the king of Assyria and send him home. There he will be killed."

The Assyrian king sent a threatening letter. Hezekiah took the letter to the Temple and had a prayer meeting. God sent him an answer through Isaiah: "I will do as you have asked. The Assyrian army will stay away from Jerusalem."

That night God sent his angel of death to the Assyrian camp, and thousands of soldiers died. Then the Assyrian king went home. But while he was worshipping his idol, some of his sons assassinated him.

DAY 227

Hezekiah's Life Is Lengthened

2 Kings 20; 2 Chronicles 32

King Hezekiah fell ill. Isaiah said, "You must prepare yourself because God has said you are going to die." Hezekiah turned his face toward the wall and cried, "Oh, Lord! Please remember me."

As Isaiah left, the Lord said to him, "Go back and tell Hezekiah that I have heard his prayer."

Isaiah hurried back and told Hezekiah, "The Lord is going to heal you! You will be well enough to worship at the Temple. And God will let you live another fifteen years."

Hezekiah said, "Give me a sign that the Lord will heal me."

Isaiah answered, "Shall the shadow move backwards or forwards?"

Hezekiah asked for the shadow to move back ten steps and the Lord performed this sign.

King Hezekiah became very rich and powerful, but he forgot to give God the credit. He acted as if he had done it all himself.

So Hezekiah used his extra fifteen years very unwisely. He was selfish and proud, and his people slipped back into idol worship. Isaiah and another prophet, Micah, tried to warn Hezekiah and the people, but they wouldn't listen.

269

Jeremiah is Put Into a Well

Jeremiah 27; 38

As Jeremiah walked around wearing the yoke, the leaders of the city became angry with him. They asked the king to kill the prophet. "His gloomy messages are bad for morale. He sounds like a traitor."

The king said they could punish Jeremiah, so they let him down into a deep, dark, muddy well.

One of the king's men told him what the leaders had done to Jeremiah. "He will starve down there, and he is the Lord's prophet. What they have done is cruel."

The king sent some men to get Jeremiah out of the well. They hauled him up to the surface. They didn't let him go but kept him in the prison.

Ezekiel Teaches Object Lessons

Ezekiel 1; 4–5

Ezekiel, a priest, was among the people of Judah taken away to Babylon by Nebuchadnezzar. God talked to people through his special messengers called prophets. Sometimes he talked to the prophets through dreams or visions. One day Ezekiel had a vision of God's throne and all the glory of heaven, and it made him bow and worship God.

Then God said, "I want you to warn all the captives by using object lessons. Draw a picture of Jerusalem on a piece of clay, and put a wall in front of it. Then build a fort outside the wall. Next, you must lie down in front of it and pretend to be starving. The people will know it is because of Nebuchadnezzar's attack on Jerusalem."

For the next object lesson, Ezekiel cut off his hair and beard and divided it into three parts. He burned one part, cut up one part, and blew away the third part. This showed that some people would starve when the city was burned up, some would be killed outside the city, and some would be scattered elsewhere.

173

No One Believes Ezekiel

Ezekiel 8–11

Ezekiel had another vision. He seemed to be picked up by the hair and whisked away to Jerusalem. The Lord showed him the idols his people had been worshipping, then told him to look in an inner room of the Temple.

There he saw leaders of Judah bowing down to pictures of false gods and other people worshipping the sun.

The Lord told Ezekiel he was going to punish his people by destroying their city, and that if they cried out to him he wouldn't listen or help them.

Then Ezekiel found himself being taken through the sky, back to Babylon. Ezekiel told the other captured Jews what he had seen, but they chose not to believe him. They preferred to believe the lies of the false prophets – that the people of Jerusalem would not be punished for their sins and that Nebuchadnezzar would never burn the city and the Temple.

God's Special Messenger

Ezekiel 12

Ezekiel wrote down everything God told him, then acted it out to the people. For the next object lesson he made a hole in the back wall of his house at night and pretended he was moving out. He took some of his belongings with him. "This is like a play on a stage," he told them. "King Zedekiah will try to get away from Jerusalem, but he will be caught and brought back here as a prisoner."

Then Ezekiel acted as if he was badly frightened. This showed how scared the people of Jerusalem would be when the attack came. God even revealed to Ezekiel what day these things would happen.

When Jerusalem was conquered three years later, Ezekiel's fellow captives realised he had been telling the truth.

DAY 236

God Sends Good News

Ezekiel 37

God still loved Israel and Judah. He gave Ezekiel more messages to encourage the people and give them a promise for the future. First God gave Ezekiel a vision of a big field covered with human skeletons. God told Ezekiel to say to the bones, "Listen to what God is going to do. He will put flesh on you and let you breathe and become alive!"

As Ezekiel watched, those words came true. Flesh grew on the bones, and the bones joined together and became human forms. Then Ezekiel called to the wind to blow on the bodies and put breath into them. Immediately the bodies came to life and were like a huge army.

God said to Ezekiel, "This shows what is going to happen to Israel and Judah. They will receive new life and strength and will become powerful again."

God told Ezekiel to pick up two sticks and name one of them Israel and the other one Judah. As Ezekiel held the sticks in his hand, they became one stick. This showed that the two countries would join together again, as in the days of David and Solomon.

The Beautiful City is Burned

2 Chronicles 36; Jeremiah 52

Back in Jerusalem, King Zedekiah sent for Jeremiah. "I want you to tell me the truth about what is going to happen," the king said. Jeremiah answered, "If I do, you will probably kill me!"

"I promise not to kill you," the king said.

Jeremiah said, "If you and your people surrender peaceably and become Nebuchadnezzar's slaves, you will be kept from harm, and the city will be saved."

Zedekiah was afraid to do that, so he held out against Nebuchadnezzar. The Babylonian army kept attacking Jerusalem. No supplies could get into the city, so the people were in danger of starvation.

Zedekiah tried to escape, but he was captured and taken to Nebuchadnezzar. As Zedekiah watched, Nebuchadnezzar killed Zedekiah's two sons and then blinded Zedekiah. He spent the rest of his life in a Babylonian prison.

The Babylonian army looted Jerusalem and burned down the beautiful Temple, the palaces, and the homes. They smashed the walls of the city and killed many of the people. The rest of the people became slaves in Babylon. The history of the kingdom of Judah came to a sad end because of the people's sin and indifference to God.

Judah - a Lonely, Deserted Country

2 Kings 25; Jeremiah 40–43

Nebuchadnezzar told his army general to be kind to Jeremiah. The general released Jeremiah and said, "You may go with me to Babylon, where you will be treated well, or you may stay here."

Jeremiah decided to stay, so the general gave him a supply of food and some money. Jeremiah stayed with Gedaliah, the governor Nebuchadnezzar had appointed.

A few of the people of Judah ran away when they knew Nebuchadnezzar was going to capture the city. But after the war, Gedaliah was left in charge, so the people of Judah asked if they could come back. Gedaliah said, "Yes. Obey the king of Babylon, and everything will go well for you."

After a while the Ammonites had Gedaliah killed, and the rest of the people were afraid Nebuchadnezzar would punish them because of Gedaliah's death. They asked Jeremiah what they should do.

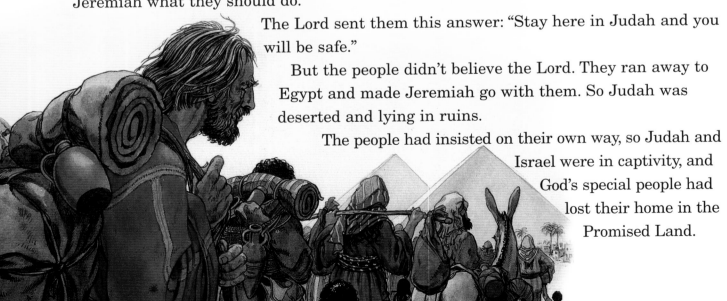

The Lord sent them this answer: "Stay here in Judah and you will be safe."

But the people didn't believe the Lord. They ran away to Egypt and made Jeremiah go with them. So Judah was deserted and lying in ruins.

The people had insisted on their own way, so Judah and Israel were in captivity, and God's special people had lost their home in the Promised Land.

Daniel and His Friends

Daniel 1

Daniel lived in Jerusalem. He loved his parents, and he obeyed everything they taught him about worshipping God and following the Law. When Nebuchadnezzar destroyed Jerusalem, Daniel was one of the captives taken to Babylon. The king chose some of the smartest and strongest boys from Judah to go to a special school where they would spend three years studying important subjects.

Daniel was one of the boys chosen, along with three of his best friends – Shadrach, Meshach, and Abednego.

Nebuchadnezzar didn't care about God. He expected the boys to do wrong things sometimes. But when they were offered food and wine that had been used in idol worship, the boys asked to be excused from eating it.

Their teacher said, "If you become weak and sick, the king will punish me."

Daniel said, "Just give us plain vegetables and water for ten days. We'll be fine."

Daniel and his friends went on to become the wisest students of all. And God gave Daniel the special gift of understanding dreams.

DAY 240

The King Has a Scary Dream

Daniel 2

Nebuchadnezzar gave Daniel and his friends good jobs and made Daniel one of his special counsellors. One night the king had a frightening dream. When King Nebuchadnezzar awoke, he knew his dream had been scary, but he couldn't remember what it was about. This worried him. The king asked his magicians and astrologers to tell him what he had dreamed, but they couldn't.

They said, "Tell us what you dreamed, and we'll tell you what it means."

The king answered, "I told you – I can't remember. Tell me what I dreamed, and I will reward you. If you can't tell me, I'll kill you!"

His wise men still couldn't answer him, and this made the king furiously angry. They said, "What you ask is impossible. Nobody in the world can tell people what they dream."

The king ordered all his wise men to be brought before him. Daniel and his friends were in the group. When Daniel heard why the king was so angry, Daniel told him he would be able to tell the king about the meaning of his dream, but first he needed time to pray. That night God gave him the answer in a vision.

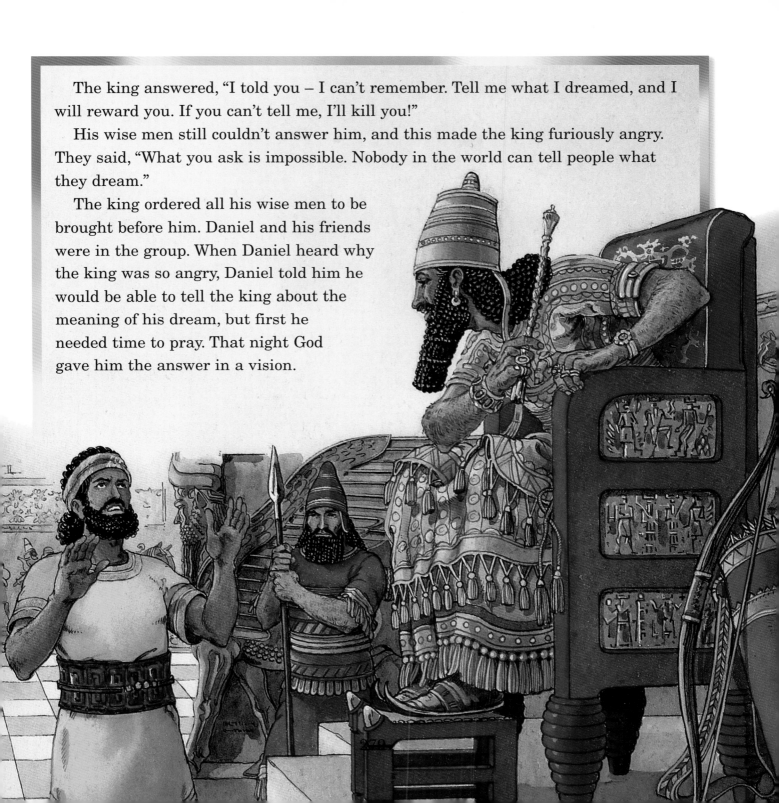

The Dream and Its Meaning

Daniel 2

The next morning Daniel said to the king, "Don't kill the wise men. Only God can explain your dream. God has told me about it because he wants you to know his message.

"You dreamed about a huge statue. Its head was made of gold, its chest and arms of silver, the middle part was bronze, the legs were iron, and the feet were of iron and clay mixed together.

"You saw a rock roll down the mountainside and smash the statue. Then the rock grew bigger until it filled the whole earth."

Then Daniel explained what the dream meant. "The statue is you. You are the head of gold. But after your kingdom is gone, another kingdom will take its place. It will be less powerful, just as silver is not as great as gold.

"Then the bronze kingdom will rule. It will be followed by another, like the iron legs. Then the iron kingdom will divide and be like the mixture of iron and clay.

"The stone stands for a great kingdom that will destroy all the others. It will come from God."

The king was grateful to Daniel. King Nebuchadnezzar made Daniel a ruler assisted by his three friends.

"We Will Not Bow to the Statue"

Daniel 3

Nebuchadnezzar built a big statue, ninety feet high and nine feet wide. He sent a message to the leaders in the country, "When you hear the band play, everyone must bow and worship the statue. Anyone who doesn't will be thrown into a hot furnace."

The band played, and everyone bowed to the statue. Daniel wasn't there, but Shadrach, Meshach, and Abednego refused to bow down.

Some of the government leaders came to the king and said, "Those young men who came as captives from Judah aren't bowing down to your statue. Are you going to let them get away with it?"

The king called the young men and yelled at them, "Don't you respect me? Don't you know I can throw you into the furnace?"

They answered quietly, "O king, even if you do put us into the furnace, our God will take care of us. Even if he should let us die, we would never worship anyone but our God. We will not bow to your statue."

How Many Men in the Furnace?

Daniel 3

When the three young men refused to bow to the statue, the king became even angrier. He shouted, "Heat up that furnace seven times hotter than before. Tie these men up, and throw them into the fire!"

283

The soldiers obeyed, but the fire was so hot that it burned them when they threw in the three men. As King Nebuchadnezzar watched, he saw something very strange. "I thought we put three men into the furnace. Now I see four men walking around in the flames. They don't even seem to be hurt by the fire."

The king came as close to the furnace as he could and called to the men, "Shadrach! Meshach! Abednego! You servants of the Most High God, come out of the furnace."

When the men stepped out, everyone could see that even their hair wasn't singed. King Nebuchadnezzar was so amazed that he made a new announcement. "I command that from now on, if anyone in this country says anything bad about God, he will be killed, and his house will be pulled down."

Then he promoted Shadrach, Meshach, and Abednego to higher positions in his government.

Another Strange Dream

Daniel 4

Later King Nebuchadnezzar had another strange dream. He told Daniel, "I saw a tree so tall that everyone in the world could see it. It had beautiful leaves and fruit. An angel came and said, 'Cut down the tree. Leave the stump in the ground where it will be soaked with rain. Let this "tree" eat grass like an animal and have a mind like an animal's; then everyone will know how great God is.'"

Daniel knew what the dream meant, but he didn't want to tell the king. The king begged him to tell, so finally Daniel said, "O king, you are the great tree. But your kingdom will be taken away, and for seven years you will act like an animal – soaked with rain, living outdoors, and eating grass. Only when you admit how great God is will you be healed and get your kingdom back."

Nothing happened for

285

a year, and the king refused to give God credit for the good things that happened to him. The angel said, "It's time for the dream to come true." Then all the terrible things in Nebuchadnezzar's dream took place.

After seven years, he began to praise and worship God. He got his throne back and told everyone about how wonderful God is.

DAY 245

The Mysterious Hand

Daniel 5

One of the kings after Nebuchadnezzar was Belshazzar. Once Belshazzar had a big party. Everyone got drunk and behaved foolishly. Belshazzar told his servants to bring in the silver and gold cups that had been taken from the Temple in Jerusalem. The king and his guests drank wine from the sacred cups and used them in a ceremony honouring their idols!

Suddenly they saw a hand writing some words on a wall. They were frightened, Belshazzar most of all. None of his wise men could read or explain the strange words.

The queen said, "Don't get so upset. Send for the man named Daniel. His God has given him a special ability to explain things like this."

Belshazzar said to Daniel, "If you can explain these words, I'll make you a rich man."

Daniel replied, "I don't want your money, but I will tell you what the handwriting means. God is telling you that you are not fit to rule. He is going to let your enemies capture the city."

The king gave Daniel gifts and made him an important official. But that night the enemy army sneaked into Babylon and killed Belshazzar.

Daniel Keeps On Praying

Daniel 6

The new king, Darius, noticed what a wise official Daniel was, so he gave Daniel an important job in his government. The more the king honoured Daniel, the more angry and jealous the other governors became. But no one could find any fault with Daniel because he was such an honest, hardworking man.

287

One reason Daniel was so successful was that he trusted and obeyed God. He prayed three times each day, worshipping God and asking him for wisdom.

Daniel's enemies said, "Maybe we can get him into trouble for praying."

They said to the king, "We think everyone should pray to you alone for the next thirty days, and if any man prays to anyone else, he should be thrown into a pit full of lions. We've written this down as a new law. Will you sign it?"

The king felt powerful and proud. Quickly he signed the law.

Daniel heard about the new law, but he still prayed to his God as usual. His enemies were spying on him. They saw him kneeling at his open window. "Now we have him!" they gloated.

DAY 247

Thrown to the Lions

Daniel 6

When Daniel's enemies saw him praying, they rushed to the king. "O king, didn't you make a law that anyone who prays to any god but you should be thrown to the lions?"

The king said, "Yes, and no one can change a Persian king's law."

Then the men said, "Well, Daniel is breaking your law. He prays to his God every day."

The king had never intended that Daniel should be punished for praying to the God of

A Dangerous Law

Esther 2–3

One day Mordecai discovered a plot to kill Xerxes. Mordecai told Esther to warn the king. With the help of the warning the traitors were caught and punished. It was all written down in the court records, then forgotten.

Haman, the king's most powerful official, liked everyone to bow down to him. Mordecai refused to bow to

293

Haman because, as a Jew, he believed he should bow only to God. This made Haman angry – with Mordecai and with all Jews.

Haman planned to get even. He said to the king, "These Israelite captives have their own rules and laws and refuse to obey yours. We'd better get rid of them. Declare that they must all be killed, and I'll pay a lot of money into your treasury."

The king agreed, and Haman made a terrible law – on a certain day in March, all citizens should kill all the Jews they could find. They could then take those Jews' possessions for their own. Haman sent messengers out all over the country to announce the law.

When Mordecai heard about it, he was brokenhearted. Mordecai wondered what he could possibly do to save his people.

DAY 252

Mordecai Asks Esther to Help

Esther 4

Queen Esther didn't know about Haman's law. When she heard that her uncle was outside the palace crying, she sent someone to find out what was wrong. Mordecai sent a message back, telling her about the trouble the Jews were in and asking her to get the king to help.

She replied, "The king is likely to kill anyone who goes to see him without an invitation, unless he is feeling kind and holds out his sceptre. It would be dangerous for me to go."

Mordecai sent another message: "You are queen, but that won't keep you from being killed in March with the rest of our people. Perhaps this is why you were chosen as queen – so you could help your fellow Jews."

Esther asked Mordecai to pray for her and to start prayer meetings all over the city. "I will go to see the king. If he kills me – at least I will have tried to help my people." While all the Jews were praying for Esther, she worked out a plan to try to convince her husband, the king, to help the Jews get out of danger.

DAY 253
A Sneaky Plot

Esther 5–7

It was dangerous for Esther to go to the king without being invited. But her life was saved when the king held out his sceptre to her! He said, "What can I do for you?" Esther replied, "I want you and Haman to come to a banquet tonight." The king accepted, and they had a fine dinner. The king asked again, "What do you want from me?"

Esther answered, "I want you both to return tomorrow for another banquet."

Haman bragged about his invitation to his family and said, "I would be completely happy if it weren't for Mordecai."

Haman's wife said, "Build a gallows and get the king's permission to hang Mordecai tomorrow. Then you can enjoy the banquet."

296

That night, the king found the record of how Mordecai had saved his life. He realised he had never rewarded Mordecai. When Haman came to see him, to ask about killing Mordecai, the king spoke first. "Haman, how could I honour someone special?"

Haman assumed the king meant him. He said, "Give him a robe and a crown. Let him ride your horse through the city. And have a prince shout, 'This is how the king honours someone who is worthy.'"

"Excellent! Do all these things for Mordecai!"

DAY 254

The Brave Queen Saves Her People

Esther 7–10

What a shock for Haman! That night he and the king went to Esther's second banquet. Again the king asked Esther what she wanted. Esther said, "O king, please save my life and the lives of all the Jews in your kingdom, for we are to be killed."

"What do you mean?" the king cried. "Who would dare to threaten your life?"

"Haman has ordered all Jews to be killed – and I am one of them!" she answered.

The king was terribly angry and left the room to think about the problem. Haman was afraid. He threw himself across Esther's couch to beg for mercy. The king came back in and thought Haman was trying to hurt Esther, so the king ordered Haman's death.

Haman was hanged on the gallows that he had built for Mordecai!

The king gave Haman's job as prime minister to Mordecai, but he could not change the law about killing Jews.

So Esther said, "Since you cannot change the law, will you make another one permitting the Jews to fight back?"

Xerxes said yes, and when the Jews were attacked, they fought back, and their lives were saved.

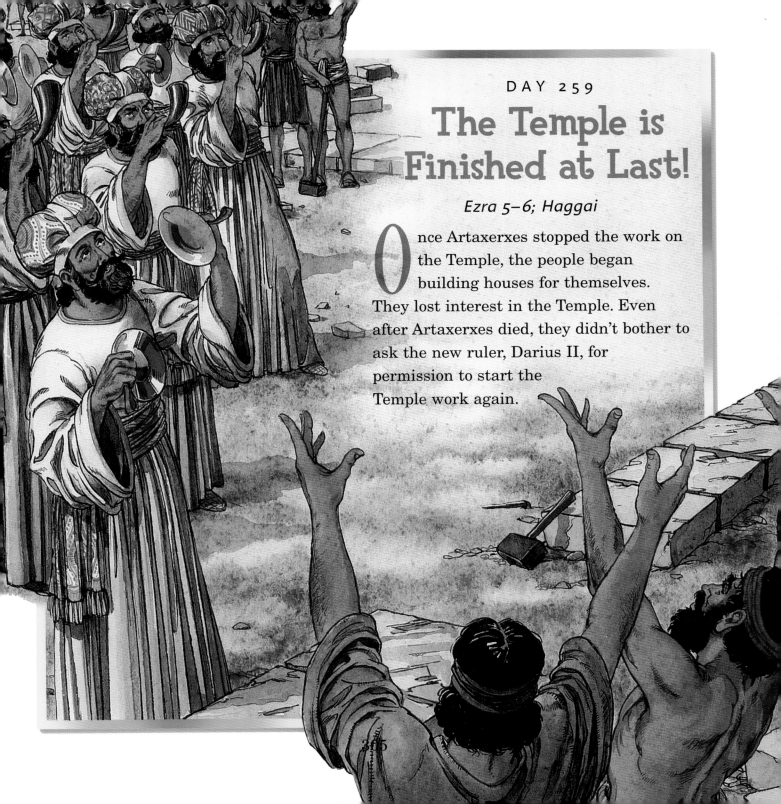

The Temple is Finished at Last!

Ezra 5–6; Haggai

Once Artaxerxes stopped the work on the Temple, the people began building houses for themselves. They lost interest in the Temple. Even after Artaxerxes died, they didn't bother to ask the new ruler, Darius II, for permission to start the Temple work again.

Their selfishness disappointed God. He warned them through his messengers, the prophets Haggai and Zechariah.

Haggai said, "You are neglecting the Temple and thinking only of your own comfort. God's house is still in ruins, so get to work!"

The people were ashamed. They started work on the Temple immediately. The Samaritans said, "Who said you could work on the Temple again?"

The leaders replied, "King Cyrus sent us to take care of God's house."

The Samaritans wrote to Darius and said, "Did King Cyrus really tell these people to rebuild the Temple?" Darius checked and found Cyrus's decree. He wrote, "You Samaritans must let the Israelites get on with their work, or I will punish you. And you must give them part of the tax money you owe me."

So the people of Judah were able to finish the Temple and celebrate the feast of Passover in their new house of worship.

DAY 260

Joyful Celebration

Nehemiah 8–13

The time of captivity for the people of Judah was over. Many of them had returned to live in their own land. The walls of Jerusalem were built, and the Temple had been rebuilt, so they could worship and serve God in his own house. They had even brought back the gold and silver bowls and cups and other treasures that had been stolen from the old Temple.

The Israelites had several celebrations to show their joy. When the walls were finished, they had a parade around the top of the wall. Then they marched to the Temple and made sacrifices to God.

They also had a thanksgiving celebration called the Festival of Trumpets. During that time Ezra read the Book of the Law aloud to everyone. He read for hours, and the people stood and listened. They all told God they were sorry for disobeying him and that they would try to do better.

Next, they signed a paper, making promises: "We will obey God, not mingle with the heathen tribes, not marry ungodly women, give the Lord a tenth of our money and grain, and keep the Sabbath day a holy day of rest."

"We will obey God, not mingle with the heathen tribes, not marry ungodly women, give the Lord a tenth of our money and grain, and keep the Sabbath day a holy day of rest."

Many Years of Trouble

Secular History

The people of Israel were back home, but they were not really free. They paid taxes to the Persian kings, who still ruled them. During the next four hundred years, one government followed another, but the Jews were always servants. The Greeks, the Egyptians, the Arameans – each ruled the Jews for a time. Then for about a hundred years they became free again, while a family of Jewish leaders, called the Maccabees, kept invaders out of Judah. Once more the people could worship God in their Temple.

But soon the Jews neglected to worship God and fought among themselves. So God let another foreign army conquer them. This time it was the Romans. The Roman emperor sent a soldier named Herod to be king of Judah. Herod was cruel, and the people hated him. He tried to make friends with the people by rebuilding the Temple, which by now was five hundred years old and in bad condition. Herod spent nine years rebuilding it, and made the Temple really beautiful.

But the Jews were still unhappy under Roman rule. They longed for a great leader to come and free them!

THE NEW TESTAMENT

A Surprise for Zechariah

Luke 1

Zechariah was a priest in the newly rebuilt Temple. He and his wife, Elizabeth, were disappointed that they had had no children and that now they were too old. The priests took turns doing each task in the Temple. One day it was Zechariah's turn to burn incense in the Holy Place. As he did this, he saw an angel beside the altar.

The angel said, "Don't be afraid, Zechariah. I have good news. You and Elizabeth are going to have a baby boy! You must name him John and bring him up in a certain way: He must never drink any wine.

"The Holy Spirit will live in him. He will bring people back to God and get them ready for the promised Messiah."

Zechariah was amazed. He said, "How can this happen? My wife and I are too old to have a baby."

"Because you don't believe," the angel replied, "you will become unable to speak until after the baby is born!" When Zechariah came out of the Holy Place, he couldn't say a word. But he showed everyone by his hand motions what he had seen and heard in the Temple.

A Promise from an Angel

Luke 1

God sent the angel Gabriel to Nazareth with a message for a young woman named Mary. Mary was a virgin; that is, she had never slept with a man. She was engaged to be married to Joseph, a local carpenter.

Mary was startled when the angel suddenly appeared in her room. Gabriel said, "Mary, you have been chosen for a great honour." Mary was troubled by his words.

He continued, "Don't be afraid. You will soon become pregnant, and when your baby boy is born, you will name him Jesus. He will be very great and will have the throne of his ancestor David. His kingdom will never end."

Mary was puzzled. She said to Gabriel, "How can I have a baby? I'm a virgin!"

The angel replied, "You will become pregnant by the power of the Holy Spirit. Your baby will be the Son of God. Your cousin Elizabeth is pregnant, too, even though she is beyond the age for having babies. Nothing that God promises is impossible!"

Mary answered joyfully, "I'm God's servant, and I'm glad to do whatever he wants me to do."

"Don't be afraid. You will soon become pregnant, and when your baby boy is born, you will name him Jesus. He will be very great and will have the throne of his ancestor David. His kingdom will never end."

313

Elizabeth Has a Baby Boy

Luke 1

When Elizabeth was about six months pregnant, Mary visited her. As Mary entered the house, Elizabeth's baby leaped inside her, and Elizabeth was filled with the Holy Spirit.

She said to Mary, "You are a fortunate woman. God has chosen you because you believe and are willing to obey."

Then Mary said, "Praise God because he has chosen me, a simple village girl. He's going to put down rulers and lift up lowly people. He has promised to be faithful to Abraham's children forever."

Mary went home after three months. Elizabeth had her baby, and she and Zechariah did as the angel had told them.

The neighbours thought they should name the baby after Zechariah, but Elizabeth said, "No, he is to be named John."

They asked Zechariah, and he wrote, "His name is John!" Immediately Zechariah got his speech back again!

He said, "The Lord is going to send us a Saviour. My child shall be a prophet of God, preparing the way before the Saviour."

Once John grew up, he spent a lot of time in the desert, until it was time for him to speak God's messages.

DAY 265

God Sends His Son

Luke 2

Joseph and Mary got married. Shortly before the baby came, the Roman emperor said everyone must go to his or her family's hometown to be counted. Joseph and Mary both came from David's family, so they had to register in Bethlehem. Bethlehem was crowded with people, and all the inns were full. The only space they could find was in a shed with some animals.

315

That night Mary's baby was born. She wrapped her little boy in warm clothes and put him in a manger.

At first, the only people who knew what had happened were some shepherds. They saw many angels in the sky and heard them say, "Glory to God! Peace on earth! A Saviour has been born today in Bethlehem. You will find him warmly wrapped and lying in a manger!"

After the angels had disappeared, the shepherds said, "Let's go and see!"

They found the little baby with Mary and Joseph. Everything was just as the angels had said. After they had visited the baby, the shepherds went out and told everyone the news.

Mary thought about what had happened and wondered what it all meant.

DAY 266

Simeon and Anna

Luke 2

The Law told new parents to dedicate their first baby boy to God. When the baby was eight days old, the parents were to name him. Mary and Joseph named their baby Jesus because that is what the angel had told Mary to do.

Later, they travelled to Jerusalem and took baby Jesus to the Temple. At the Temple they saw an old man named Simeon. He spent a lot of time in the Temple because God had told him he would not die until he had seen the baby who would become the Messiah — the Saviour.

As soon as Simeon saw the baby Jesus, he knew this was the One. He took Jesus from Mary and prayed, "O Lord, now I can die in peace. I have seen the baby who will bring your salvation to the world."

317

318

Anna lived in the Temple. She was very old and had been a prophet for many years. She, too, recognised Jesus as the Messiah. She thanked God for the Saviour, then hurried to tell everyone she met that the Messiah had been born.

The Wise Men

Matthew 2

Far away in another country, some wise men saw a bright new star. They knew it was a sign that a great king had been born. They wanted to take gifts to him, so they decided to follow the star until they found him.

After they had travelled for many days, they arrived at Jerusalem. They asked everyone, "Where is the new king of the Jews? We have been following his star because we want to worship him."

King Herod heard about them, and he was worried. Was some new king going to take away his throne? Could these foreigners be talking about the Jewish Messiah?

Herod asked the wise men when they had first seen the star. He told them to go ahead and find the baby king. "Then come back and tell me where he is, so I can worship him too," Herod said.

The star led the wise men to the house where Mary, Joseph, and Jesus were staying. The men bowed to Jesus and gave him valuable gifts – gold, frankincense, and myrrh.

Then they had a dream in which God said, "Don't go back to Herod. Take a different road home."

DAY 268

Hiding from Herod

Matthew 2; Luke 2

When King Herod found that the wise men had left without reporting to him, he was angry. He sent soldiers to Bethlehem to kill all little boys younger than two years old.

But God sent an angel to warn Joseph. "Take Mary and Jesus to Egypt, and stay there until I say it is safe to come back."

Joseph kept his family in Egypt until King Herod died. Then Joseph had a dream in which God said, "You can safely go back now." They went to live in Nazareth, where they had lived before.

Jesus grew to be a fine, strong boy. Once, when he was twelve, he was in Jerusalem with his parents for the Passover. When the group from Nazareth started home, Jesus stayed behind.

After a while Mary and Joseph missed him and went back to look for him. They found him in the Temple, talking with the teachers of the Law, who were surprised by his wisdom.

Mary said, "Son, how could you cause us such worry?"

Jesus answered, "I thought you would know I'd be in my Father's house!" Then he went home with them and was always an obedient son.

John Baptises Jesus

Matthew 3; Mark 1; Luke 3

John and Jesus were cousins. John had been chosen to prepare people to receive the Messiah and to announce his coming. John told the people, "You must be sorry for your sins and take care of the poor and the hungry. I baptise people in water, but the Messiah will baptise you with the Holy Spirit."

People asked John, "Aren't you the Messiah?"

"No," he answered. "He will come later. He's so great that I'm not worthy even to untie his shoes!"

One day Jesus came to the Jordan River. John called out, "Look! There is the Lamb of God – the Messiah!"

Jesus asked John to baptise him. John answered, "No! I'm the one who should be baptised by you!" But Jesus insisted. So John baptised Jesus in the river.

Just as Jesus came up out of the water, the heavens opened. God's Holy Spirit, looking like a dove, came down and lighted on Jesus. Then the voice spoke from heaven: "This is my dear Son, whom I love. I am greatly pleased with him."

Satan Tempts Jesus

Matthew 4; Mark 1; Luke 4

After Jesus was baptised, he went into the wilderness. He ate nothing for forty days and nights. While Jesus was weak from hunger, Satan came to him. Satan said, "If you're really the Son of God, turn these stones into bread."

Jesus answered, "The Scriptures say we don't live just by eating bread. We live by obeying every word God says to us."

Satan took Jesus onto the roof of the Temple in Jerusalem. Satan said, "Jump off! That will prove to everyone that you are the Son of God. The Scriptures say God will send angels to keep you from being hurt."

"What it really says," Jesus answered, "is that we should not test God in such a foolish way!"

Satan tried once more. He took Jesus to the top of a high mountain. They could see all the kingdoms of the world.

Satan said, "I'll give you these kingdoms to rule if you kneel down and worship me."

Jesus said, "Get out of here, Satan. The Scriptures say, 'You must worship and obey the Lord God, and not anyone else!'"

Satan gave up and went away.

DAY 271

Jesus' First Miracle

John 2

Jesus asked some men to leave their work and travel around with him. He taught them important things, so they were called his disciples. One day he and his disciples were invited to a wedding in Cana. Jesus' mother, Mary, was there too. Unfortunately, the wine was all gone long before the celebration was over.

Mary spoke to Jesus about it, but he said, "Don't expect me to do anything about it. It isn't time yet for me to do miracles." Mary didn't argue with him, but she said to the serving men, "If Jesus tells you to do something, do it."

There were six large waterpots in the kitchen. Jesus said to the servants, "Fill each of these pots with water." The servants obeyed. "Now," Jesus said, "take some of it to the host."

The host tasted what they gave him. "This is excellent wine!" he exclaimed. He said

The Woman at the Well

John 4

As Jesus sat by a well in Samaria, a woman of the village came with her pitcher. Jesus asked her for a drink. She said, "That's a surprise. You Jews don't usually speak to Samaritans."

Jesus said, "If you knew who I am, you would ask me for living water!"

"Living water?" she echoed. "You don't have a rope or a pail. How could you get water?"

Jesus replied, "The well water leaves you thirsty. But the water I give satisfies you forever."

"Then give me some," she said.

"First go and get your husband," said Jesus.

She hesitated. "…I don't have a husband."

Jesus said, "You have had too many husbands. And you are not married to the man you live with now."

The woman was embarrassed and changed the subject. "Why do you Jews worship in one place and we Samaritans in another?"

Jesus answered, "It's not important where we worship but how. Remember, salvation will come through the Jews."

"When the Messiah comes," she answered, "he will tell us everything."

"I am the Messiah!" he said.

The woman called everyone to come and meet Jesus. He preached to them for two days.

Jesus Heals a Sick Boy

John 4

Many people in the Samaritan village believed that Jesus was the Saviour. Then Jesus and his friends moved on to Galilee. They stopped in Cana. A rich government officer from Capernaum approached Jesus and begged him for help. The officer said, "My little boy is very sick and about to die. Please, come to Capernaum and heal him."

Jesus sighed. "You people always want to see miracles before you will believe in me." The child's father said again, "Please, sir! Come and heal him before it is too late!" Jesus said, "Go back home now. Your little son has been healed!"

The officer believed Jesus and started for home. His servants hurried out to meet him. "Oh, master, good news! Your son is not going to die. He has recovered!"

The happy father asked his servants, "When did he start to get better?"

They answered, "About one o'clock yesterday afternoon." The boy's father realized that was the exact time at which Jesus had told him his son was healed.

From Fishermen to Followers

Matthew 4; Mark 1; Luke 5

Jesus was walking by the Sea of Galilee. He watched the fishermen and noticed two brothers, Simon and Andrew. Jesus called to them, "If you were working with me, you would be fishing for men instead of fish!"

He said the same thing to two other brothers, James and John, who were fishing with their father, Zebedee. All four brothers listened to what Jesus was teaching.

Such crowds came to hear Jesus that he hardly had room to move. He got into Simon's boat and said, "Push the boat out a little way, and I'll speak to the people from there."

After Jesus had finished preaching, he said, "Now let's go out where it's deeper, and you can get some fish."

Simon answered, "We tried all night but couldn't find any. But if you say so, we'll try again."

They threw their nets out, and they caught so many fish that the nets broke from the weight. They were awed and a little bit afraid at what Jesus had done.

Jesus asked both pairs of brothers to leave their fishing business and become his disciples. All four men came immediately.

Jesus Heals the Sick

Matthew 8; Mark 1; Luke 4

Each town had a small place of worship called a synagogue. Whenever a famous speaker came to town, he was invited to teach there. The people of Capernaum asked Jesus to speak in their synagogue.

While he was there, a demon-possessed man called out, "Go away, Jesus of Nazareth! You've just come to make trouble for us because you are the Son of God!"

Jesus said, "Be still! Come out of him!" The demon threw the man to the ground, but it left him alone after that. From then on the man was normal.

The crowd was excited. "Imagine that! Jesus has the power to make demons come out of people!"

Then Simon took Jesus and the other followers to his home. They found that Simon's wife's mother was very sick with a high fever. Jesus went to her bedside and told the fever to leave her. She felt better immediately and got up and cooked a meal for Jesus and his friends.

That evening many other sick and demon-possessed people came and asked to be healed. Jesus healed each one.

Down Through the Roof!

Matthew 9; Mark 2; Luke 5

A paralysed man wanted Jesus to heal him. Four of his closest friends made a kind of stretcher-bed, and they carried him to the house where Jesus was staying. When they saw the huge crowds, they decided to lift the stretcher up onto the flat roof, take out some of the tiles, and lower their friend into the room where Jesus was healing people.

They made a hole in the roof, then carefully eased the stretcher down until their friend was lying right in front of Jesus!

Jesus was pleased when he saw the faith of the man's friends. Jesus said to the paralysed man, "I forgive your sins."

The religious leaders, who didn't like Jesus, said, "Who does he think he is? Only God can forgive sin."

Jesus knew what they were thinking. He said, "Which do you think is harder – to forgive sin or to heal the body? Well, I'll do both!" He said to the paralysed man, "Stand up; you are well. Now go on home."

The man jumped to his feet, picked up the stretcher, and hurried home. Everyone was absolutely amazed!

Jesus and the Sabbath

John 5

One Sabbath day Jesus passed Bethesda Pool. Many sick people waited there because when the water moved, the first person into the pool was healed.

A man was there who had been sick for thirty-eight years. He was too weak to move quickly into the pool. Jesus healed him and said, "Get up, roll up your mat, and go home."

When the religious leaders saw the man, they said, "Carrying that mat is work. You are breaking the Law by working on the Sabbath."

The man replied, "I don't know his name, but the man who healed me told me to carry it."

Later Jesus saw the man again and warned him not to go on being a sinner. Then the man told the leaders who had healed him.

The leaders scolded Jesus for not respecting the Sabbath laws. Jesus said, "My Father does good things for people no matter what day it is. I do as he does."

The leaders were shocked that Jesus called God his own father. Jesus continued, "If you don't honour the Son, you dishonour the Father. Whoever listens to what I say and believes God sent me shall have life forever."

DAY 280

The Twelve Special Disciples

Mark 2–3; Luke 6

Jesus and his followers were walking through a field on the Sabbath. Some of them were hungry, so they picked some grain, rubbed the husks off, and ate the kernels. The Pharisees said that rubbing the husks from the grain was like doing farm work, which was forbidden on the Sabbath.

Jesus said, "I have been made master of the Sabbath. I should know what is permitted and what is not!"

This made the leaders even angrier. They began to plan to kill Jesus. Jesus took his followers back to the Sea of Galilee, and he healed many sick people.

One day Jesus went alone into the desert to pray. When he returned, he chose twelve of his followers to be an inner circle of companions and helpers. They would travel with him, preach, and help heal the sick.

The twelve special disciples were Peter (the new name Jesus gave Simon the fisherman), Andrew (Peter's brother), James and his brother John, Philip, Bartholomew, Thomas, Matthew (who had been a tax collector), another man named James, Thaddaeus, Simon, and Judas Iscariot.

Jesus Preaches on a Mountain

Matthew 5; Luke 6

Everywhere Jesus went, people crowded around him. He decided the best way to speak to so many people was to climb up high on a hill. That way everyone would be able to see and hear what went on.

One time when he taught on a mountain, he was teaching his disciples, but everyone wanted to hear.

We call this the Sermon on the Mount. Jesus told the people how to be happy and enjoy God's blessing.

Be humble, not proud and stubborn.

Be sorry for your sins.

Be meek and listen to other people's opinions.

Be eager to do right.

Be kind to everyone else.

Be pure in your hearts, thinking only about good things.

Be peaceable and help others not to quarrel.

Then he said something that sounds very strange: "Be glad when others are mean to you because you believe in me and obey me! God will give you a great reward if you suffer for being my followers."

Jesus Tells How We Should Live

Matthew 6; Luke 6

In his rules for being happy, Jesus said a lot about being good. Here is a list of some of his instructions:

Be like a bright light, helping people see how good God is.

Do all the good things God told Moses in the Law.

Do not hate anyone, for hatred is like murder in the heart.

Settle your arguments quickly.

Men and women must have only pure thoughts about one another.

Married couples must not get divorced.

If you make a serious promise, you must keep it.

Be generous with others, even if they treat you unfairly.

Be just as nice to your enemies as you are to your friends.

Don't show off when you do generous things for others.

Don't show off when you pray, but do it privately.

Give your money generously to people in need, and God will take care of your needs.

Don't worry about what is going to happen. God is in control of your life.

Two Different Houses

Matthew 7; Luke 6

Jesus told his listeners not to be too quick to criticise other people but to check up on their own lives too. He promised that when they asked for God's help, he would always answer their call.

One of the most important things Jesus said was, "Do for other people the things you would like them to do for you!"

Jesus told a story. He said, "If you listen to what I say and obey my rules, you will be like a man who built his house on a rock. Heavy rainstorms came, the wind blew, and floodwater washed against his house; but it stood firm because it was built on a solid foundation.

"But if you hear what I tell you and do not pay any attention to my instructions, you will be like a man who built his house on sand. When the rain and wind and floods came, his house fell down with a mighty crash. It was a complete wreck because it had a poor foundation."

All the people who heard Jesus talk were surprised at how well he taught. They said, "We think God has given him authority to speak."

One of the most important things Jesus said was, "Do for other people the things you would like them to do for you!"

Jesus Shows Great Power

Matthew 8; Luke 7

A Roman who was friendly to the Jews paid to have a synagogue built in Capernaum. The Roman's servant became very sick, so the Roman sent word to Jesus asking him to come and heal his servant.

Even before Jesus got there, the Roman hurried out to meet him. "Master," he said, "I'm not good enough to have you enter my home. You can heal my servant without seeing him. Just speak the word, and he will be well."

Jesus said to the people around him, "This man has more faith than any Jew I know!" And he said to the Roman, "Go home. Your servant is healed."

When the man got home, he found the servant entirely well.

Later, Jesus saw a funeral procession in Nain. A widow's only son had died, and she was heartbroken. Jesus' heart was touched. He said to her, "Don't cry." Jesus stopped the procession and touched the casket.

"Young man! Come back to life!" The boy sat up and was able to talk and walk. Jesus led him to his mother. Everyone was amazed. People said, "This man is a great prophet. He can do the works of God!"

Showing Love to Jesus

Luke 7

One day a Pharisee invited Jesus to dinner. A sinful woman came to see Jesus. She brought an expensive jar of perfume. She was crying because she was sorry about her sins. Her tears fell on Jesus' feet, and she wiped them away with her hair. Then she poured the perfume on his feet to show her love and respect for him.

Simon the Pharisee thought Jesus couldn't be a prophet, or he would have known how bad the woman was and wouldn't be letting her touch him.

Jesus knew what Simon was thinking. Jesus said, "Simon, if a man lends five hundred dollars to one person and five thousand dollars to another and then tells them they don't have to pay the money back, which debtor will love him more?"

Simon answered, "The one who owes him the larger amount."

Jesus said, "When I came to your house today, you didn't wash the dust from my feet – but this woman washed them with her tears. You didn't give me a kiss of greeting – but she kissed my feet. You didn't give me oil for my head – but she poured expensive perfume on my feet.

"She is a sinful woman, but I am forgiving her sins because she loves me so much."

DAY 286

A Story about Money

Luke 12

A man called to Jesus from the crowd, "Master, I wish you would tell my brother to divide our father's money fairly." Jesus replied, "Don't ask me to settle your arguments! Besides, money won't make you happy.

"Listen. One year a farmer had such good crops that he became rich. His barns were full, so he built bigger ones. The farmer thought he would be able to relax and have fun. He thought he'd be so rich that he'd not ever have to worry about money again!

"But that night God warned him: 'You are a fool! Tonight you will die, and then what will become of your riches?'"

Jesus said, "Don't waste time worrying about money, clothes, or food. Birds don't plant crops and build barns, yet God provides food for them. Aren't you more valuable to God than birds?

"And the flowers don't make cloth and sew clothes for themselves – but see how beautifully God dresses them! If God takes care of flowers, won't he take care of you? Spend most of your time thinking about God, and he will give you everything else you need!"

A Story about Seeds

Matthew 13; Mark 4; Luke 8

Jesus told stories that taught lessons, like this one: "A farmer went out to plant his seed. Some seed fell on the path. People walked on it, and birds flew down and ate it. "Some of the seed fell on rocky soil. It started to grow, but there wasn't enough dirt to nourish the roots, so the little plants died.

"Some seed fell among weeds. The weeds were stronger than the grain seedlings, and the seedlings died.

"And some seed fell on good, rich soil. It grew tall and strong. At harvest time the farmer reaped a hundred times more than he had planted!" The disciples asked him what the story meant. Jesus said, "The seeds are God's words. Some of his messages come to hard hearts, and the devil steals them away.

"Some of the messages come to shallow hearts. These people believe for a while, but then they lose interest. Some people's hearts are like a weed patch – other interests come in and crowd out God's truth. But some people are like the rich soil. They listen and believe God's words. Then the message grows and produces fruit – many times more fruit than was 'planted'!"

A Story about Faith

Matthew 13; Mark 4

Jesus said, "A mustard seed is tiny, but it grows into a very large plant. Faith is like that. If you believe even a little bit, your faith can grow and become strong." Then he said, "Once a farmer planted some good seed in a field. But some enemies came into his field and planted weeds among his good seeds. The weeds grew big and strong along with the good grain. The farmer's servants said, 'Master, did you know your field has a lot of weeds among the grain?'

"'Yes,' he said, 'An enemy did that.'

"'Shouldn't we pull up the weeds?' they asked.

"'If you do that,' he replied, 'you will pull up grain along with the weeds. Wait until harvest time. Then the reapers can separate the weeds from the grain.'

"That's the way it is with my kingdom. The good seed is like the people who have faith in me. The weeds are like those whom Satan has planted among my people. But one day the angels will take out all my true people. Then the ones who are wicked unbelievers will be destroyed."

Two Wonderful Miracles

Matthew 8; Mark 4–5; Luke 8

Jesus and his disciples were crossing the Sea of Galilee when a terrible storm blew up. The disciples thought the boat would sink. Jesus was sleeping soundly despite the storm. The disciples woke him up, yelling, "Master! Save us or we'll all drown!"

Jesus got up and spoke to the wind and the waves. "Stop! Be still!" Instantly the wind stopped and the sea was calm.

Jesus said, "Why were you afraid? You don't have much faith!"

On the other side of the lake they saw a man who had evil spirits living in him. He was naked, and he screamed and hurt himself with stones. Everyone in town was afraid of him.

The demon in the man cried out to

Jesus, "Don't hurt me! I'm one of the many demons here. Let us go into the pigs over there."

Jesus said, "All right. Leave the man, and go into the pigs."

When they did, the large herd of pigs jumped into the lake and was drowned.

The man sat quietly with Jesus, acting perfectly normally. He wanted to join Jesus' group, but Jesus said, "No. Go home and tell your family and friends what has happened to you."

DAY 290

Jesus Gives Health and Strength

Matthew 9; Mark 5; Luke 8

Jairus was a religious leader. He begged Jesus to come to his home and heal his twelve-year-old daughter, who was dying. Jesus agreed, but on the way, a woman who had been sick for twelve years reached out and touched Jesus' robe. Immediately she was healed.

Jesus knew something had happened. Jesus asked his disciples, "Who touched me?"

They said, "Master, many people are bumping against you!"

Jesus said, "This was different. I felt healing strength go out from me."

The woman admitted that she was the one and that she had been healed. Jesus said, "You are well because you believed in me!"

As the group came near Jairus's house, a messenger came and said, "Sir, your little girl is dead."

Jesus said to Jairus, "Don't worry. She'll be all right. She's only sleeping."

The mourners were sure she was dead, and they laughed at Jesus. He took Peter,

350

Later, Jesus asked them, "What were you quarrelling about back there?"

They didn't want to talk about it, but Jesus already knew the answer because he could always tell what people were thinking and saying.

Jesus said, "Listen! If you want to be great, you must become a servant to other people. If you want to be first, you must be willing to be last."

Then he picked up and held a small child in his arms. "If you welcome a little child because of your love for me, then you are welcoming me and my Father. Don't act so proud and selfish: Believe in me the way little children do. And never hurt a child. People who are cruel to children would be better off if they had never been born."

A Really Good Neighbour

Luke 10

One day a man asked Jesus, "Master, how can I be saved?" Jesus answered, "You know the Law. What does it say?" The man said, "It says to love God and my neighbour." "Then do it," said Jesus.

"But who is my neighbour?" the lawyer asked.

Jesus said, "One day a man was travelling from Jerusalem to Jericho. Robbers attacked him. They stole his clothing and left him badly hurt.

"A priest came along, but he ignored the injured man and hurried by. Then came a Levite, or Temple worker. He didn't stop either.

"Then came a Samaritan. Samaritans don't usually like Jews. But this Samaritan took care of the man and bandaged his wounds.

"The Samaritan put the injured man on his donkey, took him to a hotel, and paid for a room where he could recover. The Samaritan told the owner he would pay more later if the money wasn't enough."

Jesus asked, "Which of the three men who saw the victim on the road acted like his neighbour?"

The lawyer said, "The one who took care of him, of course."

"That's right," Jesus answered. "Now, you do the same for others. That's the way to 'love your neighbour.'"

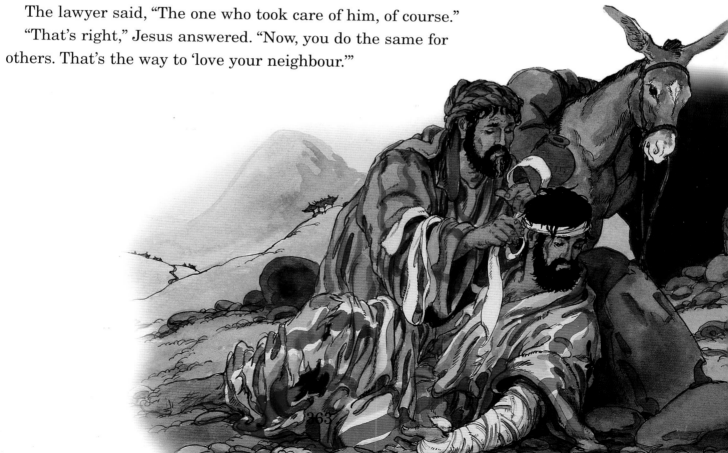

Learning to Pray

Luke 10–11

Jesus had good friends in Bethany – two sisters, Mary and Martha, and their brother, Lazarus. When Jesus visited them, Martha wanted to prepare fancy meals for him. She wanted her sister to help her, but Mary preferred to sit and listen to Jesus talk. Martha became angry with Mary. She said to Jesus, "I wish you would tell my sister to come and help me with the cooking."

Jesus said, "Learning about God is more important than food, Martha. Mary has made a good choice."

Later Jesus taught his disciples this prayer:

"Our Father in heaven, your name is holy and should be respected by everyone. We want your kingdom to come. We want people on earth to do what you want, just as the angels in heaven do.

"Please give us the food we need today. Forgive our sins, just as we forgive the sins of people who do wrong to us. Don't let us be tempted to do evil things, but keep us away from sin. You are the glorious and powerful ruler. Amen."

A Blind Beggar

John 9

One day Jesus and his disciples saw a beggar who had been blind all his life. The disciples asked Jesus, "Is this man blind because he has sinned or because of his parents' sins?"

Jesus answered, "Neither. His blindness is an opportunity for God to show his glory and power."

Jesus mixed up a sort of clay by spitting on some dirt. He put it on the blind man's eyes and said, "Go and wash it off in the pool of Siloam."

The blind man obeyed. Immediately he could see.

People looked at him and said, "Isn't this the blind beggar?" Some thought he was. Others weren't sure.

The man himself said, "Yes, I am the one who was blind, but now I can see."

"How did this happen?" people asked.

The man explained what Jesus had done.

The people looked for Jesus, but they couldn't find him.

The man's friends said, "We had better take you to the Pharisee leaders to be examined.

Open Eyes, Open Heart

John 9

The Pharisees asked the formerly blind man how he had been healed. He told them everything Jesus had done. They said, "He did it on the Sabbath, so he can't be a very good man! Who do you think he is?"

The man said, "He is a prophet!"

The leaders still doubted the man, so they asked his parents, "Is this really your son who was blind?"

"Yes," they said. "But we don't know how our son received his sight. He can tell you." They were afraid of the Pharisees.

Jesus' enemies talked to the man again. "Give God the credit for healing you, not Jesus. He is a sinner."

366

The man answered, "All I know is that I was blind before, but I can see now."

The Pharisees kept questioning him. Finally the man became angry. "Why do you keep asking me about it? Do you want to believe in him too?"

Then the Pharisees scolded the man and banned him from the synagogue.

Later Jesus asked him, "Do you believe in God's Son?"

"I would if I knew who he was," the man answered.

"I am the One," Jesus said.

Then the man said, "I do believe in you!"

DAY 303

Jesus is Our Shepherd

John 9–10

Jesus said, "I have come to make blind people see – and to make some people who think they can see realise how blind they are!" The Pharisees asked if he was speaking about them. Jesus answered, "If you knew you were blind, you would not be sinful; but because you think you have such good eyes, you are guilty of sin!" Then Jesus said, "If a person climbs over a fence into the sheep pen, we know he is a thief. The one who enters through the door is the real shepherd. His sheep know him. "I am like a good shepherd to those who love me. I am willing to sacrifice my life for my sheep. I know my sheep, and they know me."

Then Jesus talked about God, his Father. "My Father loves me because I give up my life and will get it back again."

The Pharisees were shocked and angry when Jesus said God was his Father. They even thought an evil spirit was controlling him.

367

"I am like a good shepherd to those who love me. I am willing to sacrifice my life for my sheep. I know my sheep, and they know me."

But people who had seen his miracles said, "Look at the good things he does for people! How could he heal a blind man if he had a demon?"

Jesus' Good Friend Dies

John 11

One day Lazarus became very sick. His sisters, Mary and Martha, were afraid he might die, so they sent word to Jesus, asking him to come and heal Lazarus. Jesus didn't rush to Bethany at once. He said, "The purpose of this illness is not Lazarus's death; it is intended to bring glory to me, the Son of God." And he stayed away from Bethany for two more days.

At last he said, "Let's go to Bethany now. Lazarus has gone to sleep, and I must wake him up."

At first his disciples didn't understand, but then he said, "Lazarus is dead, and when you see what I will do, you will believe in me."

Martha ran out to meet Jesus. She said, "Master, if you had been here, Lazarus wouldn't have died. But even now he would come back to life if you tell him to."

369

DAY 305
New Life for Lazarus

John 11

Jesus said, "Yes, your brother will rise again. I am the Resurrection and the Life. Anyone who believes in me shall rise from the dead and live forever. Do you believe this?"

Martha said, "Yes, Master. I believe you are the Messiah."

Martha went home and told Mary that Jesus wanted to talk to her. Everyone thought Mary was going to her brother's grave, so they followed her.

Mary said to Jesus, "If you had come sooner, our brother would not have died."

When Jesus saw her crying, he felt very sad, and he cried too. He asked them to take him to the grave. It was a cave in the side of a hill, with a big stone in front to seal it shut.

Jesus said, "Roll the stone away."

Martha said, "But he's been dead for four days, and his body will have decayed."

Jesus answered, "I told you I would do a miracle." Then he prayed and called out loudly to Lazarus to come out of the grave! How surprised and frightened all the people were when Lazarus appeared!

Jesus said, "Unwrap those tightly bound cloths, and let him go!" Then Lazarus went home with his sisters.

Ten Are Healed; One is Grateful

Luke 17

One day Jesus said to the disciples, "If a friend commits a sin, tell him it is wrong. If he is sorry, be sure to forgive him. Even if he does it again and again, you must be willing to keep on forgiving him."

Another time ten men who had leprosy came to meet Jesus. They couldn't come too close because everyone thought leprosy was contagious. They called out to Jesus, "Master, please take pity on us." Jesus cared about sick and hurting people. He said, "Go and show yourselves to the priest." By law lepers had to do this when they thought their disease was cured. The priest had to agree they were well before they could go home and live normally.

As the ten men walked toward the Temple, their skin became clear and healthy! One of the ten, a Samaritan, hurried back to Jesus, fell down at his feet, and cried out with joy, "Praise God! I'm completely healed!"

Jesus said, "Didn't I heal ten men? Where are the other nine? You are the only one to come back and give thanks. Because you have faith, you have been healed."

DAY 307

Healing on the Sabbath

Luke 13

This story is about a woman whose back had been crippled for eighteen years so she could not stand upright. One Sabbath day she went to her local synagogue, and Jesus was there to teach. He saw her stiff, bent back, and he felt sad about her pain.

Jesus said to her, "Woman, your back is completely healed."

As soon as he had said these words and touched her, she was able to stand up straight like everyone else! She was so happy that she praised God and thanked him.

The synagogue leader was angry because Jesus had healed someone on the Sabbath day. The leader yelled, "You have plenty of other days to heal people. You don't need to break the Sabbath!"

Jesus answered, "You take your animals from their stalls and lead them out to get water on the Sabbath day, don't you? If you do that for a mere animal, shouldn't I do a kindness for this human being – a daughter of Abraham – who has been in this terrible condition for eighteen years?"

These words made his enemies feel ashamed of themselves. And the crowds of people were happy because of this miracle Jesus had done.

Looking for the Lost

Luke 15

One day some Pharisees were grumbling about the bad people Jesus spent time with. Jesus heard them and said, "Suppose you were a shepherd with a hundred sheep to care for. If one of them wandered away from the flock, what would you do? Wouldn't you leave the other ninety-nine sheep in the sheep pen and go out to hunt for the lost one until you found it? Then you would carry it home and celebrate with your friends and neighbours. I, too, am more concerned about the one who is lost than I am about the ninety-nine who do not stray." Then he said, "If a woman has ten coins and she loses one in her home, don't you think she will look in every corner and crack and sweep the floor carefully until she finds it? Then she will be happy because she has found her valuable coin. She will call in her friends to celebrate with her. "And so the angels in heaven are happy when one sinner repents and is found by God."

The Son Who Ran Away

Luke 15

Jesus told another story, this time about a farmer's younger son. The son was tired of helping on his father's farm, so he said, "Father, give me my share of your money so I can leave home."

The father divided his property between his two sons. The younger one took his share, packed up his clothes, and went far away from home.

He made lots of friends because he had plenty of money. But after he had carelessly wasted everything, his "friends" disappeared.

The only job he could find was tending pigs. No Jewish boy liked pigs because they were unclean. But it was the best he could do. He was so hungry he could have eaten the dry husks of the pigs' food.

He began thinking how comfortable his home had been and decided he would go back and confess to his father that he had done the wrong thing and didn't deserve to be his son anymore. Then maybe his father would let him become one of the servants.

His father hoped that his son would return home. When, one day, the father saw his son walking down the road toward him, he ran up to him, then hugged and kissed him!

DAY 310

The Runaway Returns

Luke 15

The runaway son began to explain: "Father, I have sinned against you…" But before the son could ask if he could become a servant, his father called to one of his slaves, "Bring my son some good clothes, some decent shoes, and a ring for his finger.

Kill that fat calf in the pen, and we'll have a feast to celebrate."

When the older son had finished working in the fields, he came home to hear the sound of music and fun. When he realised the party was in honour of his younger brother, he wasn't very happy.

The older son said to his father, "I've always been a good son and a hard worker, but nobody ever gave me a big party! My brother has been out wasting your hard-earned money, and when he comes home broke, you invite friends round for a celebration. You've even killed the best calf!"

His father said, "Don't be angry. You are my dear son, and everything I have is yours. But we should be happy because my son who was lost is found."

The Rich Man and the Beggar

Luke 16

The Pharisees were very proud, and they loved being rich. One day Jesus told them this story: "A rich man lived in a large, expensive home. He had beautiful clothes and everything else he wanted. At his gate lay a poor dirty beggar, begging money from passers by. His name was Lazarus. He was covered with sores, and he didn't have proper food.

"Lazarus died. Angels took him to heaven, so he was with Abraham. Then the rich man died too, but he went to the place of fiery torment called hell. The rich man could see up into heaven, where Lazarus was now happy and comfortable.

"The rich man called to Abraham, 'Please send Lazarus down here to relieve my suffering.'

"Abraham answered, 'You had every comfort when you were on earth. Poor Lazarus had nothing. Now it is the other way around.'

"The rich man cried out, 'Please send Lazarus back to warn my brothers so they can escape this place.'

"But Abraham said, 'They have the Scriptures to warn them. If they won't believe them, they won't believe someone who comes back from the dead.'"

DAY 312

Jesus Loves Little Children

Matthew 19; Mark 10; Luke 18

Jesus loved children. One day while he was teaching the people, some mothers brought their children up close to Jesus because they wanted him to give the children a special blessing.

The disciples thought they shouldn't interrupt Jesus while he was talking, so they scolded the women and tried to get them to leave.

Jesus stopped the disciples at once. "Don't send them away. Don't prevent children from coming to me. They are the very ones for whom my kingdom is intended. Everyone who wants to be in my kingdom should be like these little children – pure and trusting and loving."

Then he picked the children up and held them in his arms. He often warned people never to do any harm to a child. Children are important to Jesus, and he loves them very much.

379

Jesus Heals Bartimaeus' Eyes

Matthew 20; Mark 10; Luke 18

A blind man named Bartimaeus lived near Jericho. One day he heard that Jesus was coming, and he knew that Jesus often healed people with serious problems like his. Bartimaeus couldn't see Jesus, of course, but he sat by the side of the road and called out, "Jesus, Son of David, please have mercy on me! Oh, Son of David, have pity on me!"

Some of the people around him became cross. "Oh, do be quiet!" they growled.

He called out all the louder, "Please, Jesus, help me!"

When Jesus finally heard him, he said, "Tell that man I want to talk to him."

"Come on, Bartimaeus," the people said. "Jesus wants to see you."

Jesus asked Bartimaeus, "What do you want me to do for you?"

Bartimaeus replied eagerly, "Oh, Teacher, I want you to give me my sight!"

"All right," said Jesus, "it's done. Your faith has healed you." From that moment Bartimaeus was able to see perfectly!

The Man in the Tree

Luke 19

A nother man in Jericho was eager to see Jesus. Zacchaeus collected taxes for the Roman government. The people hated the Romans, so they disliked Jews who worked for the Romans. Tax collectors were especially hated because most of them were dishonest.

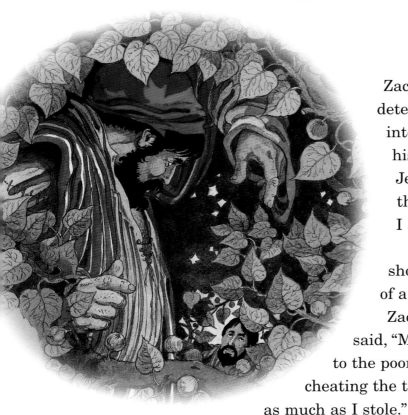

Zacchaeus was very short. He was so determined to see Jesus that he climbed into a sycamore tree. When Jesus and his disciples came near to the tree, Jesus looked up and spoke directly to the little man: "Zacchaeus, come down; I am going to your home today."

Some people in the crowd were shocked. "Look! He's going to the home of a terrible sinner!" they muttered.

Zacchaeus welcomed Jesus gladly. He said, "Master, I want to give half of my money to the poor. And since I got some of my riches by cheating the taxpayers, I will give back four times as much as I stole."

Jesus could see that Zacchaeus' faith had changed his heart. Jesus said, "I came to look for lost people and save them. Today salvation has come to this house."

DAY 315

Crowds Welcome Jesus to Jerusalem

Matthew 21; Mark 11; Luke 19; John 12

Jesus decided to go to Jerusalem. First he stopped in Bethany to visit Martha, Mary, and Lazarus. Then he sent two of his disciples to a nearby town to find a donkey's colt on which he could ride into the city. They brought the animal and put their coats on it to make it more comfortable for Jesus.

As he rode into Jerusalem, great crowds of people gathered to welcome him. They put their coats and branches of palm trees down on the road. They shouted their welcome to him: "God bless the Son of David! He comes in the name of the Lord!"

Jesus went into the Temple. When he saw merchants and moneychangers cheating the people, he shouted, "My Temple should be a place of prayer, but you have turned it into a robbers' den!" And Jesus drove them out of the Temple.

Jesus healed sick people in the Temple. Children called out, "God bless David's Son!" The leaders were angry and asked Jesus if he heard what they were saying.

"Yes," he said. "The eighth psalm says that babies and children shall praise the Lord!"

DAY 316

The Farmer's Son

Matthew 21; Mark 12; Luke 20

Jesus taught in the Temple every day. This is one of his story lessons: "Once a rich farmer had a large vineyard. He rented it out and left town. At harvest time he sent a man to get his share of the grapes. But the renter beat the man up and wouldn't give him anything.

"The owner sent another helper, but the same thing happened. The owner even sent a third one, but he, too, was beaten and chased away.

"Then the owner thought, 'If I send my own son, surely they will respect him, and I'll get my share of the crop.' But when his son got there, the tenant farmers said, 'He will inherit the farm. If we kill him, we can keep the land.' So they attacked and killed the son."

Then Jesus asked, "What do you think the owner will do then? He will come and kill those wicked renters and find new people to take care of his farm." The Temple

leaders realised they were the tenant farmers of Jesus' story and Jesus was the owner's Son, whom they were planning to kill. They wanted to arrest him, but he was so popular with the people that they didn't dare.

DAY 317

Clothes for a Wedding

Matthew 22

Jesus knew he would not be with his followers much longer. He wanted them to be ready to get along without him. He told them this story lesson: "A king's son was about to be married. He invited many friends to the wedding feast, but

kingdom. Jesus said to them, "Anyone who wants to be the most important must become unimportant. The way to be a leader is to be a servant!"

Jesus Washes the Disciples' Feet

John 13

Jesus showed the disciples exactly what he meant when he said a leader must be a servant. He asked them, "Who is greater, the master or the servant?" Of course they said, "The master!"

Jesus said, "Well, I am the master of this feast, but I am also your servant."

Then he took a basin of water, stooped down, and washed the disciples' feet and dried them with a towel.

Peter said, "Lord, I don't want you to wash my feet!"

Jesus answered, "If I don't, you won't really belong to me."

"Then wash every part of me!" Peter said.

"That isn't necessary, Peter," Jesus said. "If I have washed your feet, you are clean all over. But that isn't true of everyone in this room." He knew that one of the disciples was going to betray him.

Jesus said, "Do you understand what I just did? If I, the Master, have washed your feet, how much more important it is that you wash one another's feet. I've given you a good example; now follow it."

390

The Last Supper

Matthew 26; Mark 14; Luke 22; John 13

John asked Jesus what he meant when he said one of them was not loyal. Jesus said, "It will be the one to whom I give this piece of bread after I dip it into the bowl." He handed the bread to Judas Iscariot and said, "Go and do what you have to do."

Then Satan made Judas even more determined to betray Jesus. Judas left and went out into the night.

Jesus said, "I won't be with you much longer. I want to give you a new commandment. You must love one another as I have loved you! It will show the world that you belong to me."

Then Jesus took a piece of bread and broke it. "This is my body, which will be broken for you. When you eat this bread, you will show my death to everyone."

Next he took a cup of wine and blessed it. "This wine is my blood, poured out for you so God will forgive your sins. Drink this in memory of me."

Jesus said his followers should do this over and over until he returns to earth again.

Jesus Prays in the Garden

Matthew 26; Mark 14; Luke 22; John 13–14

Peter said, "I love you so much that I would even die for you!" Jesus shook his head sadly, "Peter. Before the rooster crows tomorrow morning, you'll say three times that you don't even know me!"

Jesus promised that while he was gone the Holy Spirit would live in them and comfort them. Then they went to the Garden of Gethsemane for prayer. Jesus took Peter, James, and John with him to a private place. He said, "Wait here and pray."

As Jesus prayed alone, he thought about how terrible his death would be. He prayed for a while, then went back and found the disciples sleeping. Jesus said, "Can't you stay awake and pray for me?"

He went back to pray some more. His heart was in such pain that he sweated drops of blood. Jesus cried out, "Father, if it is possible, keep me from this death. However, I want to do your will, not my own."

He returned to the disciples and again he found them asleep. This time he just said, "Go on sleeping. You need your rest."

DAY 326

Soldiers Arrest Jesus

Matthew 26; Mark 14; Luke 22; John 18

Jesus prayed a while longer; then he went back to Peter, James, and John. He said, "Get up now. Judas is coming to betray me." They all jumped up and saw a group of soldiers and Temple officials coming through the garden. The soldiers had lanterns and torches and were carrying weapons.

Jesus knew what was going to happen, but he asked, "What do you want?"

They answered, "We've come for Jesus of Nazareth."

He said, "I am the one you want."

Peter was so angry with Jesus' enemies that he grabbed his sword and cut off the ear of the high priest's servant, Malchus.

Jesus said, "Put your sword away, Peter. Shouldn't I do whatever the Father requires?" Then Jesus healed Malchus's ear.

Jesus said, "You come after me as if I were a robber. Why didn't you arrest me when I was teaching in the Temple?"

The soldiers arrested Jesus and took him to the high priest.

DAY 327

Peter Hears the Rooster Crow

Matthew 26; Mark 14; Luke 22; John 18

As the soldiers took Jesus away, Peter followed. While Jesus was being questioned inside the house, Peter waited in the courtyard. A servant girl looked at Peter. She said, "I think I've seen that man with Jesus."

Peter was afraid, so he said, "No! I don't even know him."

Later another person looked at him closely and said, "Yes, this man is a disciple of the man from Nazareth."

But again Peter said, "I certainly am not!"

A third person said, "He must be one of Jesus' people. He talks like a Galilean."

Peter was more frightened than ever, and he shouted, "You don't know what you are talking about! I've had nothing to do with that man Jesus."

As he said those words, Jesus was being led across the courtyard. Jesus turned and looked at Peter, and then a rooster crowed!

Immediately Peter remembered that Jesus had said Peter would deny that he knew him three times before the rooster crowed. Peter cried because he was ashamed

A Crown of Thorns

Matthew 27; Mark 15; John 19

Pilate's soldiers mocked Jesus. They made a crown of thorns, and they pushed it onto Jesus' head. Pilate hoped he could get the religious leaders to leave Jesus alone. He said again. "He really doesn't deserve to die."

But the leaders said, "If you don't let us crucify him, we'll tell the emperor that you let one of his enemies escape!"

So Pilate stopped objecting and said, "You may crucify him. But I don't think he is guilty!"

Judas, who had betrayed Jesus, was sorry for what he had done. Judas took back the thirty pieces of silver the religious leaders had paid him.

He said, "I don't want your money. I did the wrong thing when I betrayed the Lord."

The religious leaders just laughed at him and said, "That's too bad! It's too late now!"

Judas was so sad about turning against Jesus that he took his own life by hanging himself.

The Crucifixion

Matthew 27; Mark 15;

Luke 23; John 19

The soldiers made Jesus carry the heavy wooden cross up a hill called Calvary. Jesus stumbled under the heavy weight. Then the soldiers got a man from the crowd to carry it for him.

Jesus lay down on the cross. They hammered nails through his hands and feet and stood the cross upright.

There Jesus hung, in great pain, for several hours.

He prayed that his heavenly Father would forgive his enemies. "They don't understand what they are doing," Jesus said.

The soldiers divided up his clothes. They rolled dice to see who would get his robe.

Pilate had told them to put a sign on the cross over Jesus' head saying "Jesus of Nazareth, the King of the Jews."

Two criminals were crucified at the same time as Jesus, and one of them believed in Jesus. The criminal said, "Please remember me when you have your kingdom."

Jesus answered, "This very day you will be with me in heaven!"

Jesus Dies on the Cross

Matthew 27; Mark 15; Luke 23; John 19

Jesus' family and friends stood near the cross. His mother, Mary, and the other women who were his followers were there, as well as the eleven disciples. Jesus said to the disciple John, "John, treat Mary as if she were your own mother." And he said to Mary, "John is to be like your son."

Jesus suffered most because he was dying as a sinner even though he had never done anything wrong. He did it to accept the punishment that should have been ours.

Jesus was very lonely as he died. He cried out, "O my God, why have you left me?"

The sky turned dark, even though it was early afternoon. Jesus said he was thirsty, and someone gave him a taste of sour wine.

Then he cried out loudly, "It is finished!" And he

401

died. At that moment an earthquake shook the ground. The curtain in front of the Most Holy Place in the Temple was torn from top to bottom. One of the Roman soldiers near the cross said in amazement, "Why, this man really was God's Son!"

DAY 333

Jesus is Buried

Matthew 27; Mark 15; Luke 23; John 19

One day after the crucifixion was the Sabbath, so the religious leaders wanted Jesus' body removed from the cross before the Sabbath began. The religious leaders said, "Be sure all the men you crucified are really dead; then take them down."

When the soldiers looked at Jesus, they saw that he was already dead.

A man named Joseph of Arimathea had admired Jesus very much. He had kept it a secret because he was a member of the Jewish religious council and the rest of the members were Jesus' enemies.

Joseph owned a burial cave in a garden not far from where Jesus was crucified. He asked Pilate for permission to bury Jesus' body in his tomb.

Joseph took Jesus' body, wrapped it in a linen cloth, and laid it in his tomb. Jesus' mother and the other women watched as Joseph rolled a heavy stone in front of the tomb; then they went away, feeling very sad and lonely.

DAY 334

Alive Again!

Matthew 28; Mark 16; Luke 24; John 20

Jesus' enemies asked Pilate to put guards by Jesus' tomb. "His disciples might come and steal his body and then pretend he has risen from the dead," they said. The women wanted to prepare Jesus' body for burial, but they couldn't do it until the Sabbath was over. Very early in the morning, on the day after the Sabbath, the women went to the tomb carrying the necessary spices.

When they got there, they were surprised to see that the stone was already rolled away from the tomb. They looked in and saw an angel sitting where Jesus' body had been!

403

The women were afraid, but the angel said, "Don't be afraid. Jesus is not here. He has come to life. Tell his disciples he is alive and will meet them in Galilee."

As the women hurried away, they saw Jesus in the garden. "Don't hold on to me. Go and tell my disciples that I'm alive and will see them in Galilee," he said.

When the women told the disciples, they could hardly believe it. Peter and John hurried to the tomb to see for themselves, and they found that the tomb was indeed empty!

The Disciples See Jesus Alive

Mark 16; Luke 24; John 20

The disciples could hardly believe that Jesus had actually come to life. But soon they began to see proof. Two disciples were walking to Emmaus. They were still very sad about Jesus' death. Suddenly Jesus was there with them, but they didn't recognise him.

Jesus asked them why they were so sad, and they said, "Don't you know what happened to Jesus last week? His enemies crucified him! Some of our people heard that he has risen, but how can we tell?"

Jesus talked to them for a long time, explaining all the Scriptures that told about the Saviour and how they applied to him. The disciples invited him to supper, and when Jesus broke bread they realised they had been talking with Jesus all that time!

He disappeared, but they hurried back to Jerusalem to tell everyone that Jesus was alive.

They learned that Peter had seen Jesus too. While they were talking about him, Jesus appeared to all of them! He showed them the nail wounds in his hands and feet; then he ate some supper with them.

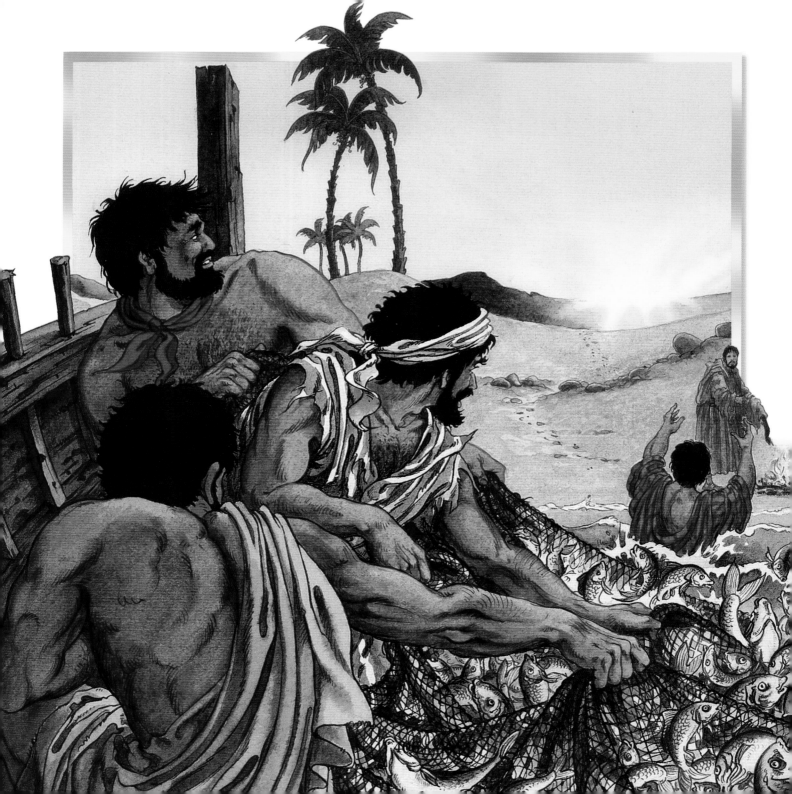

The Disciples Go Fishing

John 21

One day Peter and several other disciples went fishing. They fished all night but didn't catch anything. Toward morning they saw a man on the shore. They didn't recognise him as Jesus. He called to them, "How's the fishing?"

They answered, "We haven't caught anything!"

He said, "Throw the nets on the other side of the boat."

They did, and immediately the nets were so full of fish the men couldn't pull them aboard.

John shouted, "It must be our Lord!"

Peter swam ashore – he was so happy to see Jesus. The men dragged the net in. They had caught about 150 fish.

Jesus was cooking some fish over a small fire on the shore. After breakfast he

407

talked to Peter alone. He asked Peter if he really loved him. Peter said he did, so Jesus said, "Then you must spend your life feeding my sheep and my lambs."

He meant that Peter must tell others about what Jesus had done for them and show them how to live as faithful followers of the Lord.

DAY 337

Back to Heaven

Matthew 28; Mark 16; Luke 24; Acts 1

One day Jesus went up on a mountain with a group of his followers. He said, "God has given me all power and authority. Go and preach to people all over the world. Teach them to obey the rules and advice I have given you. When they believe in me, baptise them in the name of the Father, the Son, and the Holy Spirit. I will always be with you, to the end of the world."

Jesus told his disciples to stay in Jerusalem. In a few days the Holy Spirit would come to them and give them special power to do the things Jesus had told them.

Then he led the group toward Bethany. Jesus gave his blessing to all his friends. Then he went up into the sky until he disappeared into the clouds.

They saw an angel who said, "Why are you staring at the sky? Jesus has just gone to heaven, but one day he is going to return again!"

So the disciples waited for God to send the Holy Spirit as Jesus had promised.

DAY 338

The Holy Spirit Comes

Acts 2

Because Judas was gone, the disciples needed someone to take his place in the inner group of twelve. They made the choice by casting lots. Matthias was the one chosen to be the new disciple.

After about seven weeks, the disciples were still meeting regularly and waiting for the Spirit. One day they heard a loud noise, like the roaring of a storm. Then they saw little flames of fire over their heads, and they were all filled with the Holy Spirit.

They began to speak in languages they had never known before. People who gathered to see what was happening were amazed. Most of them thought it was wonderful, but a few laughed and said, "They've been drinking!"

Peter told the crowd. "We aren't drunk! What has happened to us is exactly what the prophet Joel predicted."

Then Peter preached about how Jesus had died and risen again to take away the world's sin. About three thousand people believed his message and were baptised – and that was the start of the Christian church.

One day they heard a loud noise,
like the roaring of a storm. Then
they saw little flames of fire over
their heads, and they were all filled
with the Holy Spirit.

Obeying God, Not Men

Acts 3–4

A man in Jerusalem had been crippled all of his life. Each day his friends carried him to the gate of the Temple where he begged for money. Peter and John went to the Temple to pray. The beggar asked them for money. Peter said, "I don't have any money, but I can give you something better. In the name of Jesus, get up and walk!"

Right away the man not only walked, but he jumped around, shouting praises to God. Everyone who saw this was amazed.

Peter told them, "Jesus gave us power to do miracles. We want all of you to become his followers!"

The religious leaders arrested Peter and John and put them into prison for preaching about Jesus. After the leaders questioned the disciples (now called apostles), they had to release them because healing the man was not illegal.

But they told Peter and John, "You must not preach anymore about this Jesus of Nazareth."

Peter and John wouldn't promise that. They said, "Jesus told us to preach, and you say not to. Should we obey God or men?"

The leaders had no answer to that question!

DAY 340
Lying to God

Acts 4–5

The believers went on telling people about Jesus. They met together for prayer and worship. They loved one another and shared what they had with poor people. Sometimes they even sold their property and put the money into a fund that everyone could use.

One day Ananias brought in some money and said, "I sold my house, and I am giving the money to the treasury." But he had really sold the house for much more money and was only pretending to share it all. God told Peter what was going on.

Peter asked Ananias, "Is this all the money you got for your house?"

Ananias lied, "Yes, that's all." Peter said, "Why do you lie? The money was yours, but you tried to deceive us." Immediately Ananias fell down dead. The men took him out for burial. Soon his wife, Sapphira, came in. Peter said, "Sapphira, did Ananias bring all the money from the sale of your house?"

"Yes," she replied, for she and her husband had agreed to lie.

"Why do you try to fool God?" She fell dead, too, and they buried her next to Ananias.

DAY 341
The Cost of Obedience

Acts 5

The Jewish religious leaders had warned Peter and John not to preach about Jesus, but Peter and John went on doing it. The Holy Spirit came and gave them courage. They healed the sick and cast out evil spirits.

and said, "I see the Son of God at his Father's right hand in heaven!"

They dragged him out of the city. They took off their robes. A young man named Saul guarded their clothing as they threw heavy, sharp stones at Stephen. He was so badly hurt that he died.

As Stephen was dying, he prayed, "Lord, don't blame them for this sin!"

DAY 343
Saul is Cruel to Christians

Acts 8

Stephen's death was the beginning of a new wave of cruelty against the believers in Jerusalem. Saul was one of the worst enemies of the church. All the believers were afraid of him.

The believers spoke about Jesus wherever they went. Philip went into Samaria, where he preached and healed people.

One day as Philip was travelling, he saw a man from Ethiopia riding in a chariot. The man was reading something, and he looked troubled. He had been reading Isaiah's prophecies about Jesus and couldn't understand them. Philip explained what Isaiah meant, and he told the Ethiopian all about Jesus.

The man asked if he could be baptised.

"Yes," said Philip, "if you truly believe."

"I do believe that Jesus is the Son of God," the Ethiopian answered. So Philip baptised him in a nearby stream.

416

Saul Sees the Light!

Acts 9

Saul decided to go to Damascus and find believers to arrest. He took some soldiers with him. As he travelled, something very strange happened. A brilliant light shone down out of heaven, and a voice said, "Saul, I am Jesus. Why are you trying to hurt me?"

"What should I do, Lord?" Saul asked.

"Go to Damascus and wait for instructions," the voice said.

The soldiers heard the voice but didn't see anyone. When the light and the voice were gone, Saul realised he was blind.

Then the Lord spoke to Ananias, a disciple in Damascus. "Go to Judas's home, in Straight Street. Ask for Saul of Tarsus. I've told him you will come and give him back his sight."

"Oh, Lord, I'm afraid! Saul is a terrible enemy of all believers."

"Don't worry. I've chosen him to be my messenger not only to Jews but to Gentiles, too!"

Ananias obeyed. He found Saul and said, "The Lord has sent me so you can receive your sight and be filled with the Holy Spirit."

And that is what happened! From then on Saul was a faithful follower of the Lord Jesus.

Can the Believers Trust Saul?

Acts 9

The news quickly spread among the Christians that their old enemy Saul was now saying he believed in Jesus. He was even preaching the gospel in Damascus. Some were glad to hear this, but others didn't trust him.

Some Jews in Damascus became angry with Saul because he said Jesus was the Messiah, God's Son. They decided to kill him. They watched the city gate, planning to capture him if he tried to leave. But the believers heard about the plot and helped Saul escape. They let him down over the city wall in a big basket!

Saul returned to Jerusalem and tried to join the believers' fellowship. But they were afraid of him. One of their members, Barnabas, knew what had happened on the road to Damascus. He took Saul to the believers and said, "Listen! You know I would not trick you. Let me tell you how Saul became a believer." Then he told them the whole story.

"He really is one of us," Barnabas said. From then on, the church accepted Saul.

believed. The judges then sent word that Paul and Silas could go free. But Paul said, "They beat us and imprisoned us without a trial. That was illegal because we are Roman citizens. Let them come and release us themselves!"

The judges had not realised the apostles were Roman citizens. They were worried that they would get into trouble, so they came and apologised and begged the apostles to leave.

Paul's Preaching Starts Trouble

Acts 18–19

In Corinth, Paul made friends with a Christian couple, Aquila and Priscilla. They were tentmakers, just like Paul. Later Paul preached at Ephesus, doing miracles and leading many to believe in Jesus. Most of the people in Ephesus had worshipped the Greek goddess Diana. They bought silver idols of Diana to keep in their homes. When they became Christians they didn't worship the idols anymore.

Soon the men who made the idols were losing business. Demetrius, a silversmith, called a meeting and said, "We are losing much business because of Paul's preaching. We must get rid of him." The silversmiths started a riot. Everyone shouted, "Great is Diana of the Ephesians!" An angry crowd tried to find Paul to attack him. But Paul's friends kept him safe.

The mayor of Ephesus got everyone's attention and said, "This isn't doing any good. If these preachers are breaking any laws, bring them before a court in the legal way. This riot will only get us into trouble with the Roman government. Calm down, and go home." The riot stopped, and the apostles were able to leave the city in safety.

More Christians and More Trouble

Acts 20–23

Once Paul was preaching on the third floor of a building. He talked until midnight. A young man sitting in an open window fell asleep and tumbled to the ground below. Everyone thought he was dead, but Paul picked him up, and

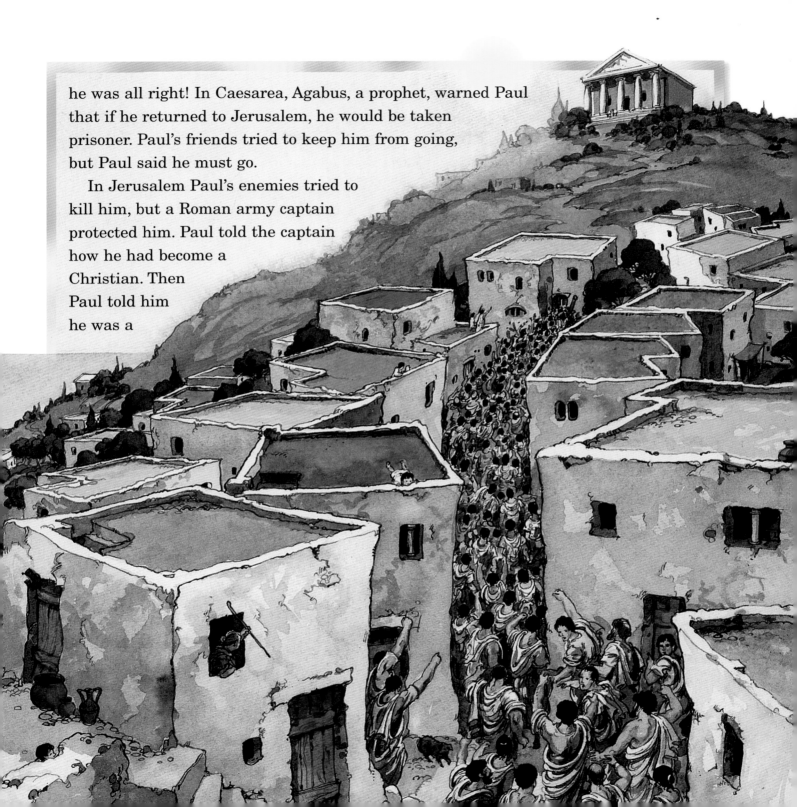

he was all right! In Caesarea, Agabus, a prophet, warned Paul
that if he returned to Jerusalem, he would be taken
prisoner. Paul's friends tried to keep him from going,
but Paul said he must go.

In Jerusalem Paul's enemies tried to
kill him, but a Roman army captain
protected him. Paul told the captain
how he had become a
Christian. Then
Paul told him
he was a

Roman citizen. A Roman citizen was supposed to get a fair trial if he was suspected of a crime. Forty of Paul's enemies vowed not to eat or drink until they had killed Paul. They planned to kidnap him, but somehow Paul's nephew heard about their plot and warned Paul and the captain. The captain decided to send Paul to the Roman governor, Felix, in Caesarea. They went secretly, at night, to protect Paul from his enemies.

Paul Talks to Felix

Acts 23–24

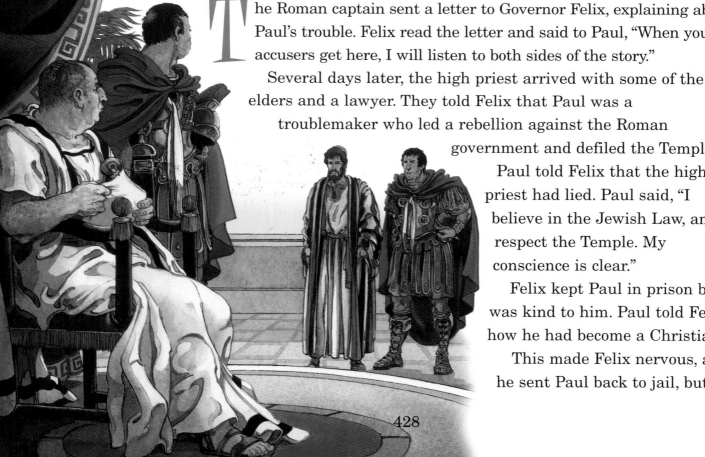

The Roman captain sent a letter to Governor Felix, explaining about Paul's trouble. Felix read the letter and said to Paul, "When your accusers get here, I will listen to both sides of the story."

Several days later, the high priest arrived with some of the elders and a lawyer. They told Felix that Paul was a troublemaker who led a rebellion against the Roman government and defiled the Temple!

Paul told Felix that the high priest had lied. Paul said, "I believe in the Jewish Law, and I respect the Temple. My conscience is clear."

Felix kept Paul in prison but was kind to him. Paul told Felix how he had become a Christian. This made Felix nervous, and he sent Paul back to jail, but

Felix talked with him often. Two years later a new governor named Festus came and took Felix's place.

Paul Appeals to Caesar

Acts 25–26

Paul's enemies tried to get the new governor, Festus, to send Paul back to Jerusalem to be tried. They thought they might have a chance to kill him before a trial could take place! But Festus refused. He said, "No, the man is in Caesarea. That is where we will try him."

Again Paul's enemies came and told lies about Paul, and again Paul denied them. Festus asked him, "Do you want to go to Jerusalem to continue this trial?"

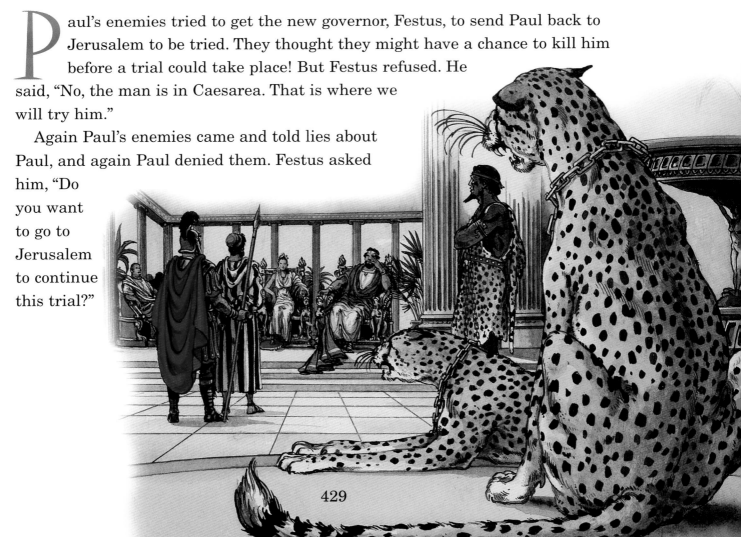

"No!" Paul said. "I have a right to appear before Caesar, the Roman emperor."

"All right," Festus replied. "You shall have an audience with Caesar!"

King Agrippa visited Festus a few days later, and Festus told him all about Paul.

Paul told Agrippa about his turning to Jesus Christ and preached the gospel to him, but Agrippa was not convinced that the gospel was true. However, he could see that Paul was innocent of any crime.

Agrippa said to Festus, "If Paul hadn't insisted on appearing before Caesar, I would have released him. But now he will have to go to Rome."

The governor made arrangements for Paul to sail to Rome, carefully guarded by some soldiers.

DAY 357

A Storm and a Shipwreck

Acts 27

Festus put an officer named Julius in charge of Paul on the voyage to Rome. Strong winds drove the ship off course. The captain stopped at Myra and transferred his passengers to another ship headed for Rome.

The weather got worse, and the new ship's captain stopped at Fair Havens for several days. It was the wrong time of year to make such a voyage, and Paul advised the captain to stay in Fair Havens until spring.

The captain disagreed and sailed anyway. The storm got worse. The winds blew the ship far out to sea. For many days the crew fought to keep the ship from sinking. Finally, they lost all hope.

When Paul wrote to the believers in Rome, he reminded them that all people are sinners but that if they would trust in Jesus Christ, God would take away their sins.

Paul told the Romans to serve God and love each other and their enemies. He taught them to obey the government and its laws.

When Paul wrote to the Corinthians, he said, "Don't quarrel and split up into unfriendly groups." He told them how to have strong marriages, being pure and loving to one another. And he said each believer had his or her own special abilities to help the church and serve other people.

Paul said that if we love others, we will be patient and kind. We won't be jealous, envious, boastful, proud, selfish, or rude. We will always be loyal and defend those we love!

In every one of Paul's letters he promised that the Holy Spirit would give believers the power to live the right kind of lives.

DAY 361

The Christian Soldier's Armour

Ephesians 6

When Paul wrote to the Ephesian Christians, he reminded them that Satan is the worst enemy of God and God's people. Satan tries to stop us from doing right. It's like a long, hard war throughout our lives.

Paul advised the Ephesians to use the armour God gave them to defeat Satan.

Paul said that truth is like the wide belt that soldiers wore to protect the middle part of the body. And right living is like a breastplate that protects the heart. Faith is the shield that stops the arrows Satan shoots at us, and salvation is the helmet that protects our heads from injury. He said we can move away from Satan quickly if we wear the shoes of the good news of peace with God.

435

But the best weapon against Satan, Paul said, is the sword of the Spirit which is the Word of God, the Bible.

And then he told them one more good way to win the battle with Satan: pray all the time!

Jesus is Coming Again

1 Thessalonians 4–5; 2 Thessalonians 2–3

Paul wrote two letters to the believers in Thessalonica, telling them about the promise that Jesus will return. He said that when Jesus is ready to return, he will appear in the sky and give a great shout of victory. An archangel will cry out loudly, and there will be a trumpet call.

The Christians who have already died will rise and be taken up into the sky to meet Jesus. After that, those on earth who love Jesus will rise into the sky too.

All believers will then be given new bodies, perfect and pure in every way, and they will be with Jesus forever.

Paul said that these amazing things will happen very quickly. He wanted everyone to know about the future so we will not worry about what happens to Christians who die. They are safe in God's care.

Paul said believers must keep watching for Jesus and obeying God as they wait for that wonderful day. Those words are just as true today as they were then.

The Runaway Slave

Philemon

Once when Paul was in prison, he had a visitor named Onesimus. Paul told him about Jesus, and Onesimus became a Christian. He did many kind things for Paul, but he had a serious problem. Onesimus was a slave who had run away from his master. Paul was surprised to hear that the master was his friend Philemon. Long ago Paul had told Philemon about Jesus and Philemon had become a believer.

Onesimus decided he should return to Philemon and be his slave again. Paul was afraid that Philemon might punish Onesimus severely for running away.

Paul wrote a letter for Onesimus to take to Philemon. In the letter Paul thanked Philemon for helping the church and letting the believers meet in his home. He asked Philemon to be kind and forgiving to Onesimus.

Paul said, "Now that Onesimus is a believer too, you and he should be like brothers. If Onesimus owes you any money, I will repay it." Then he reminded Philemon how much he owed Paul for helping him find God. Nothing could repay that debt!

DAY 364

An Unsigned Letter

Hebrews

The writer of Hebrews wrote that Jesus Christ is like the high priests of the Old Testament. The high priest went into the Most Holy Place in the Temple and offered the blood from sacrificed animals. Then God forgave the sins of the

138

people who had given those animals. When Jesus died to become our Saviour, he gave his own blood for our salvation, so God has forgiven us and we can go into his presence and speak to him in prayer.

The writer of Hebrews explained what real faith is. He said it is being sure something is going to happen even though we are not able to see it happening right now.

In Hebrews we read of people who had this kind of faith – Abel, Enoch, Noah, Abraham, Sarah, Jacob, Joseph, Moses and his parents, the Israelites who followed Moses out of Egypt, and the soldiers who marched around Jericho.

The writer said that we should live our lives as if we are running a race in a stadium and all those heroes of faith are watching and urging us on.

Day 365

John's Vision of Heaven

Revelation

The apostle John was a prisoner on the island of Patmos. One morning he had a wonderful vision of Jesus in his glory. "His eyes were bright like flames of fire," John wrote. "His feet gleamed like polished bronze, and his voice was like thunder. His face shone like the sun."

Jesus said to John, "I am the Living One who died but is now alive."

He took John's spirit into heaven. John saw God sitting on a great throne. Light flashed from him. Lightning and thunder came from the throne. In front of it was a shining crystal sea. Then John heard millions of angels singing praise to God.

John saw terrible things happening on earth to people who refused to obey the Lord. But then he saw the Holy City.